Lower Georgia Street

California's Forgotten Barbary Coast

BRENDAN RILEY

America Through Time®
ADDING COLOR TO AMERICAN HISTORY

Cover Illustrations

Front: Tom Slaight photo, Charles Gifford lithograph.
Back: Thomas W. Atkinson Jr. photo.

America Through Time is an imprint of Fonthill Media LLC
www.through-time.com
office@through-time.com

Published by Arcadia Publishing by arrangement with Fonthill Media LLC
For all general information, please contact Arcadia Publishing:

Telephone: 843-853-2070
Fax: 843-853-0044
E-mail: sales@arcadiapublishing.com
For customer service and orders:
Toll-Free 1-888-313-2665

www.arcadiapublishing.com

First published 2017

ISBN 978-1-63499-024-0

Typeset in Minion Pro 10pt on 13pt
Printed and bound in England

Contents

INTRODUCTION

Vallejo is a city with great features, active citizens, and an interesting history. Skilled residents built everything from warships with sails to nuclear-powered submarines at nearby Mare Island Naval Shipyard, the first U.S. Navy base on the West Coast and the city's main employer from 1854 to 1996. Over the years, many Vallejoans advanced to prominent positions and levels in law, medicine, education, government, religion, music, acting and other fields and disciplines; others made it to world-class levels in basketball, football, baseball, boxing, swimming, professional auto racing and other sports. In the oldest part of town, streets lined with architecturally significant homes and commercial buildings lead down to the Mare Island Strait, which divides the city from Mare Island. The strait is the last stretch of the scenic Napa River that runs into San Pablo Bay and, in turn, San Francisco Bay and the vast Pacific Ocean. So why focus on the seemingly negative by writing about Vallejo's notorious Lower Georgia Street district, once a favorite hangout for Navy sailors looking for a good time? Why dredge up stories of a rough-and-tumble past? Why not take the position of one local historian and columnist who once wrote that some of the denizens of the Lower Georgia Street district were people "of whom we shall say nothing."

But the Lower Georgia Street district dominated a significant part of Vallejo for many decades. The city's original business district, it morphed over time into a bar-brothel-gambling zone, with a handful of outliers such as a tattoo parlor, fish market, sporting goods store, laundry, grocery, sports arena, restaurants and hotels. The district changed as the community was whipsawed by significant events much larger than Vallejo. Wars started, the United States got involved, military build-ups began, and activity at the Mare Island Naval Shipyard increased. With dramatic expansions of the shipyard workforce and ship-building activity, along with arrivals of more Navy ships in need of repairs, business on the Vallejo side of the river would boom—and so would problems stemming from drinking, drugs, gambling and prostitution. All that activity would be followed by peacetime lulls or orders from top Navy brass in Washington, D.C., to shipyard commandants to clean up the problems. The Lower Georgia district would improve, but only temporarily. What happened there, like it or not, is part of Vallejo's fascinating, entertaining history, but written details about the district have been at best scattered and minimal. My focus has been to collect that information and put it in context with other less controversial aspects of Vallejo and Mare Island that have been written about previously.

The unsavory reputation of the Lower Georgia Street district was known all around the San Francisco Bay area and throughout the Navy, particularly among sailors in the Pacific. That reputation wasn't just something established in World War II. It goes back more than a century, to Vallejo's earliest days, judging from hundreds of newspaper articles, U.S. Navy and FBI documents, history books, other source material I read and interviews I conducted. I relied heavily on the newspaper accounts, which journalists like to call the first rough drafts of history. Historians prefer official documents and other primary sources to newspaper stories, and I don't disagree—providing such source material is readily available. But when it's not available, or lacks specifics, or utilizes bureaucratic phrasing that tiptoes around on-the-street realities, there's nothing quite like those newspaper stories, however raw or incomplete they might be. The same can be said about my interviews with people who witnessed the Lower Georgia Street scene, and interviews with their descendants. The following pages contain many historical highlights, but it's certain there are more tales to be shared. Hopefully this book will encourage that storytelling.

Most of us who grew up in Vallejo while the Lower Georgia Street district was still standing were admonished by our parents to avoid the district. For multi-generation Vallejoans, that admonition probably echoed the advice that your great-grandparents gave your grandparents many years earlier, when they were growing up. People wonder why Vallejo tends to get a bad rap in some circles, from residents of adjacent communities and elsewhere. The town's colorful—some would say off-color—history is at least a partial explanation. For all its good features, Vallejo had a dark side for a long time. What Vallejo and the Navy experienced with Lower Georgia Street is similar to that of almost any shipyard town, especially in war years. San Francisco's infamous Barbary Coast, 30 miles to the south, makes Vallejo's Barbary Coast look relatively tame by comparison. For that matter, scholarly accounts of ancient history relate how sailors found similar attractions when their ships sailed into Mediterranean seaports more than 3,000 years ago.

While there were repeated demands over the years to clean up the Lower Georgia Street district, there were some practical, if publicly unspoken, reasons for tolerating the gambling, drinking and prostitution. With the sailors on liberty in a few square blocks just a short ferry ride across the Mare Island Strait to their ships or barracks at Mare Island, they were easier to round up, easier to control. Authorities could look the other way if a bar scene didn't get too crazy, and send in the military police to break up the action when it got too wild. Depending on who was police chief, shipyard commandant, mayor, council member or prosecutor, or what grand jury was in session, the saloons, gambling joints and "disorderly" houses would be raided—or ignored. The pattern that can be clearly seen in the newspaper accounts and other documents dealing with the district is one of periodic crackdowns against vice, followed by stretches of relative quiet and tolerance, followed by increasing problems and more crackdowns, and on and on. There were major efforts to improve the situation, including costly construction of a naval YMCA that was dedicated by President Theodore Roosevelt and opened in 1904. A ban on any drinking within five miles of Mare Island Naval Shipyard or any other U.S. Navy shipyard in the country was ordered by the Navy during World War I. The Navy made repeated demands for a clean-up during World War II. But over time the hand-wringing and reform efforts always would slacken and the wild Lower Georgia Street scene would return.

This book isn't meant to offend anyone by digging up old stories that some would rather forget. No malice is intended. For young sailors, Marines or Army soldiers carousing on Lower Georgia Street, it was the time of their lives. For some sailors, it was their last "liberty" before their ships or submarines headed out to sea and were lost in battle, never to be seen again. For others, the low-life activity in the district was something to check out but mostly to avoid and make other choices. Leo Cullen and about 500 of his fellow soldiers in an Army regiment from Boston, stationed here during World War II, met and married local women and lived out their lives in or near Vallejo, raising families and making important contributions to their adopted city. Submarine sailor Richard Lemke met Christine Herger, his future wife, at a USO dance. Lemke's later achievements in business and civic affairs included a leading role in creating the Vallejo Naval and Historical Museum. His sister-in-law, Dorothy Herger, drew the great drawings of Lower Georgia Street that illustrate this book. Her drawings, done just before the entire district was bulldozed, represent the only complete record of what the district looked like in its final days.

For those of us who were raised in Vallejo and who served on Navy ships that anchored or tied up in distant ports, knowing what Lower Georgia Street represented was useful in deciding whether to set foot in certain bar and "red light" zones in Olongapo, just outside the Navy's Subic Bay base in the Philippines, the Wan Chai district in Hong Kong or the once-notorious Gaslamp district in San Diego. You had at least a slight edge, assuming some sobriety, over other sailors fresh out of boot camp who had never seen such sights before.

I grew up on Georgia Street, just a few blocks from the Lower Georgia Street district, and as a boy would wander around there a bit during the day. It wasn't difficult to do. Vallejo's beautiful Carnegie library, where I was supposed to be, was right on the edge of the district. In my teens, I went through the district every day, headed to a deckhand job on ferry boats that ran to Mare Island. On some weekend nights, my friends and I would look for sailors who would buy us beer. By then, many of the old buildings in the district were in bad shape and their demolition, as part of a massive redevelopment project, was already underway. One of our hangouts was the top of York Street Hill, overlooking Lower

Georgia, after all the homes that once stood there had been torn down. A century earlier, that hill had been the location of the California State Capitol. Growing up, we would hear stories about Vallejo's history, including some tales about the wild times during World War II. You never knew for sure whether to believe those tales, but the research that produced this book proved they were true—and they represented merely the tip of the iceberg.

1

Vallejo and Mare Island: The Early Days

Discussions of Vallejo's once-notorious Lower Georgia Street district always include tales of colorful, chaotic times in its many saloons and cafes, backroom or basement casinos and flophouse brothels. The district also was the scene of much violence, ranging from fistfights to knifings and shootings that left people badly wounded or dead. Racial tensions led to full-scale riots involving hundreds of sailors, Marines and Army soldiers. How the district existed as long as it did, into the late 1950s, and early 1960s, is an intriguing question. When you start looking for some of the answers, sooner or later you end up talking about tolerance, defined in most dictionaries as a willingness to put up with something—in this case the sort of activity that many Vallejoans didn't necessarily agree with.

Tolerance takes many forms, all of which seem to apply to the Lower Georgia district. Consider some synonyms for the word: acceptance, toleration, open-mindedness, forbearance, liberality, patience, charity, indulgence, understanding. Add some conditions that foster those states of mind, and the reasons for the long existence of the district become clearer. Those conditions included resignation. Over time the district got rougher and rougher but there didn't seem to be any easy way to improve it—short of bulldozing the entire area, which did finally occur. There also were pragmatic, expedient reasons for accepting the status quo. Prohibition, the Great Experiment, was a failure in Vallejo, just as it was elsewhere in the country. But if people wouldn't stop drinking, post-Prohibition licensing of drinking places at least provided some control. Prostitution would exist in any place where there were thousands of young men from all branches of the service, so decisions were quietly made to employ doctors and other medical professionals to help prevent the spread of venereal disease. Public health trumped public antipathy over red-light districts. That attitude reflected a Mare Island Naval Shipyard motto: "Our sole mission is to serve the fleet."

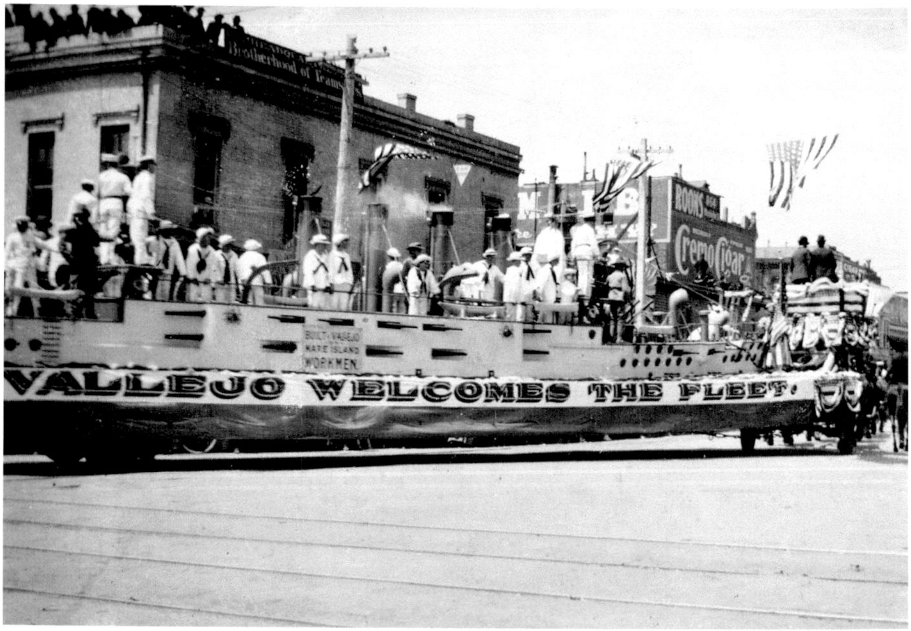

An early-1900s parade float depicting a Navy warship declares "Vallejo Welcomes the Fleet." A smaller sign says "Built in Vallejo by Mare Island Workmen." *[Vallejo Naval and Historical Museum]*

Laws against gambling came and went over the years, but gambling still was widely tolerated, no matter what was on the books. There were all types of games, ranging from keno at laundries to slot machines, craps and blackjack tables and roulette wheels in small casinos in back rooms or basements of bars. Tolerance in some cases was conditioned upon payment of bribes to ensure corrupt officials would look the other way, or would make a phone call alerting someone about an upcoming police raid. In other cases, a weak-willed official could try to avoid the issues by saying the responsibility for cleaning up the district was the job of another arm of government. Besides such blame-shifting and finger-pointing, fear was a factor. Not all police officers would enter rough joints where they might get attacked—even by the proprietor.

An argument also can be made for tolerance by Vallejo's first city leaders who, however civic-minded, had seen much violence and crime in the Gold Rush and Comstock Lode mining camps of California and Nevada. While they established stores, banks and other legitimate commercial enterprises, built fine homes and raised families in Vallejo after leaving those rough mining camps, what they experienced there may have inured them to the lawless activity in the Lower Georgia district—some of it right next door to their own businesses. Whatever the variation in the forms of toleration, they all were present at one time or another over the many decades that the district existed.

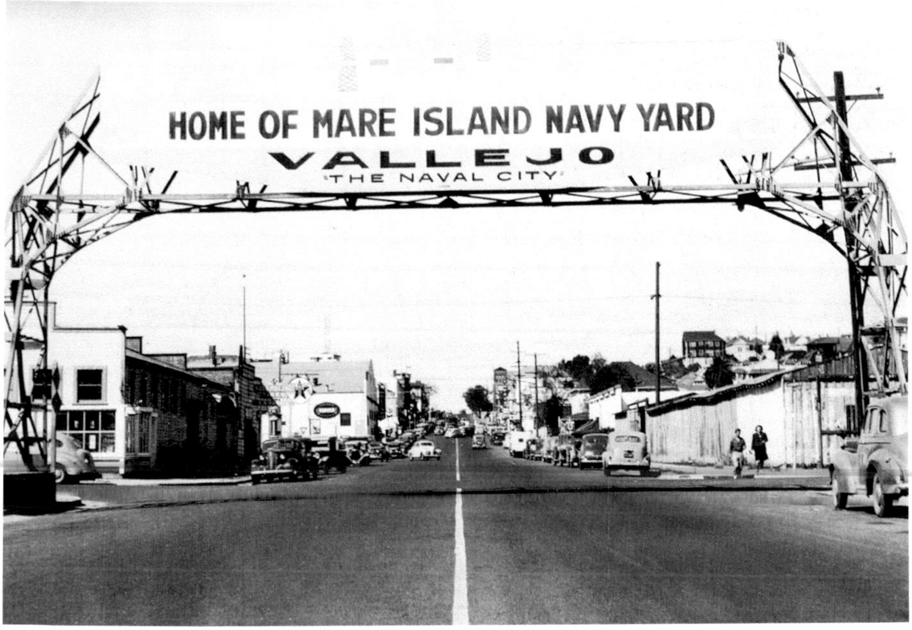

This arch across Sonoma Boulevard welcomed visitors to Vallejo in the 1940s. *[Mare Island Naval Museum]*

"Nearly every city or town has its 'past'—one that may have brought joy or sadness on its demise, depending on one's lifestyle," Wilson "Red" Buehrer, city editor at the *Vallejo Times-Herald*, wrote in a 1978 article, years after the Lower Georgia district was bulldozed. "Well, Vallejo has its very own, and some people still don't care to talk about it."

"With Lower Georgia Street in full swing in World War II and Korean War days—not to mention pre-war times—Vallejo was known throughout the Fleet as one of the best liberty towns in the Navy," wrote Buehrer, whose long career at the *Times-Herald* followed his World War II service as a Navy sailor. "The district was a neon-lit conglomeration of bars, hole-in-the-wall hamburger and Chinese food eating joints, all-night theaters, pawnshops where sailors and down-and-outers could trade for drinking money, tattoo parlors, liquor stores and upstairs hotels and rooming houses whose activities were far in advance of today's massage parlors."

"It was a rip-roaring, mini-Barbary Coast district adjoining the so-called downtown section of Vallejo," Buehrer said in describing how illegal activity continued as some authorities looked the other way. "We can remember playing slot machines in the Veterans Memorial Building on Alabama Street while city officials and their wives led the Grand March at the Police and Firemen's Ball, the social event of the season each year."

THE FIRST EUROPEANS ARRIVE

The Lower Georgia district's wild times were far off in the future when the first Europeans saw what would become the sites of Vallejo and Mare Island Naval Shipyard, the nation's first military shipyard on the West Coast. In 1772, Spaniards on an overland expedition led by Capt. Pedro Fages reached the south side of the Carquinez Strait. They could see what would become Vallejo on the north side, but didn't attempt to cross the strait to get a closer look. Three years later, on Aug. 5, 1775, Lt. Juan Manuel De Ayala, in command of the *San Carlos*, became the first Spanish mariner to enter San Francisco Bay. A few weeks later, Jose Canizares, a sailing master under De Ayala, explored the area by launch and identified the land across the Napa River from the future site of Vallejo as an island. He named it *Isla Plana*, or Flat Island.

In 1833, Mariano Guadalupe Vallejo passed through the area on his way to Sonoma, his base as *commandante* of Mexico's northern frontier. He eventually wound up with more than 170,000 acres in Mexican land grants, including the *Rancho Suscol* grant that encompassed the future Vallejo site and *Isla Plana*. The island got its current name, Mare Island, according to one generally accepted story, as a result of a mishap in the Carquinez Strait involving a white mare belonging to Gen. Vallejo. One version has the mare falling off a crude raft and ending up on the island, and another version has the mare drifting away from horses that Vallejo's workers or soldiers were swimming across the strait. After the discovery of the horse on Isla Plana, Vallejo renamed the island *Isla de la Yegua*, or Island of the Mare.

Besides getting credit for naming Mare Island, Vallejo also started the process that resulted in creation of the city bearing his name. In *General Vallejo and the Advent of the Americans*, author Alan Rosenus says Vallejo, by virtue of circumstances, training and personal philosophy, was "extremely partial to American political thought," and from the early 1840s on "his desire to make California a part of the United States became his most urgent political goal." California's first legislative session began on Dec. 15, 1849, in San Jose, prior to the formal Sept. 9, 1850, entry of the state into the Union. Vallejo, serving as a senator in that session, pushed for a permanent capital city at the south end of his *Rancho Suscol*. The proposed capital city's future seemed bright. Gen. Vallejo, considered the richest man in the state, offered 156 acres of land and $370,000 in gold to pay for construction of several government buildings. His plans called for a capitol building, state offices, state library, university, schools, hospitals, orphanages and gardens. There were few doubts about his ability to fulfill his promises.

In *The Capitol That Couldn't Stay Put*, author June Oxford said Vallejo wanted the seat of state government named Eureka, but his friends in the Legislature overruled him and decided to name the new city Vallejo, in his honor. On Oct. 7, 1850, California voters overwhelmingly supported the location, casting 7,477 votes for Vallejo. San Jose ran a distant second with 1,292 votes and 399 votes were cast for Monterey.

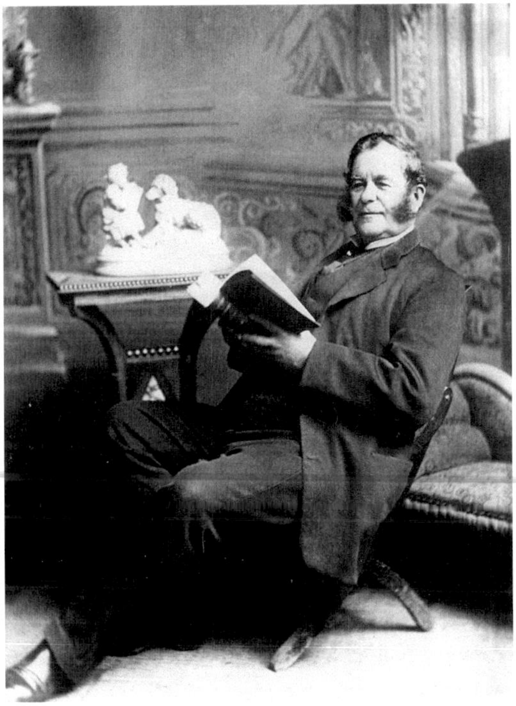

Gen. Mariano Guadalupe Vallejo was the Mexican *commandante* of northern California and owned vast tracts of land. That included the *Rancho Suscol*, the site of present-day Vallejo. *[Vallejo Naval and Historical Museum]*

California's second legislative session convened on Jan. 6, 1851, still in San Jose as Vallejo tried to complete his building project. But there were signs of trouble as the lawmakers adjourned on May 1 and started planning for their third session, scheduled to open on Jan. 5, 1852, in Vallejo. Gov. John McDougal had ordered the state offices and archives moved to Vallejo without prior legislative approval or an adequate review of the construction, and by September realized that work on the Capitol was moving slowly. He proposed a return to San Jose, but lawmakers, meeting in San Francisco a week before the scheduled start of the third session, voted twenty-eight to thirteen for Vallejo.

What the legislators encountered, despite Gen. Vallejo's valiant efforts to have the new state house ready for business, was an unfinished wood-frame building atop York Street Hill, overlooking the Napa River, with seating improvised from nail kegs or benches made by laying boards on stools. It wasn't until Jan. 8 that enough chairs arrived. The building's exterior had been hurriedly painted with a yellow wash, a treatment that produced what was described as an "orangeade" effect. There were no rostrums, committee rooms or printing facilities, and the inadequate hotel accommodations in the newly sprouted town were described by an *Alta California* correspondent as "villainous." The writer quipped that three legislators, with no place to sleep, sat in chairs until nearly frozen, then ran around to warm up and repeated the process until morning. The Assembly chambers were on the lower floor and the Senate chambers on the top floor. A bowling alley and saloon, dubbed the "Third House," occupied the basement. The steamer *Empire*, which brought many of the lawmakers to Vallejo, became a floating boarding house for about 100 people who had to trudge through tar-like mud to reach the statehouse. Legislators had been in session for only one week when they voted to leave town. On Jan. 16, the *Empire* cast off, packed with legislators and others, bound for Sacramento for the rest of the session. In her book about the roaming seat of state government, Oxford wrote that the legislators' reception upon arrival a day later included "music, oratory, cannon thunder, a parade and all the panoply the town could muster."

Vallejo had a second chance at capital city status, as a result of flooding in Sacramento that forced the legislators to commute by boat to that city's statehouse, a two-story court building. But when the fourth session of the Legislature convened in Vallejo on Jan. 3, 1853, Oxford wrote, "Vallejo's dream capital remained a magnificent mirage" and dissatisfaction with conditions multiplied. Lawmakers voted a month later to change the capital city's location and reconvened on Feb. 11, 1853, in nearby Benicia, which had offered its elegant new city hall as a meeting site. But Benicia couldn't hang onto its new status either. When the fifth legislative session convened there on Jan. 2, 1854, there were more complaints about lack of improvements, scarce accommodations and high prices. One reason for poor accommodations was that Sacramento advocates came up with a scheme to tie up available rooms: sending a couple hundred men to Benicia to rent hotel and boarding house rooms just before the lawmakers arrived. The Sacramento advocates also succeeded in pushing through a bill to make their city the capital of California. On Feb. 25, the same day that Gov. John Bigler signed the new law, legislators in Benicia voted to adjourn and meet on March 1 in Sacramento. Except for more flooding in Sacramento in 1862 that forced lawmakers to shift for a few months to San Francisco, the days of a drifting California capital were over.

Gen. Vallejo sold the Vallejo townsite for $25,000 to his son-in-law, John B. Frisbie, who was married to Vallejo's oldest daughter, Epifania. "Greater than the financial loss was the personal defeat, the disappointment in his business partners, and the disillusionment," Oxford wrote. "From then on, Vallejo restricted political office to the local level." The stark statehouse building atop York Street Hill was used for several years by local farmers for hay storage, and the basement was divided into small apartments. A fire started in one of the apartments in June 1859, spread to the hay and the entire building was destroyed in a matter of minutes. Author Rosenus says Gen. Vallejo was characterized by some as "a dream chaser" drawn to schemes difficult to realize. Rosenus added, "In reality, his ideas were sound enough, but he was a careless businessman and—when it came to relying on others—a stoic." As for Frisbie, Rosenus described him as "a born lobbyist" who "would see to it that the U.S. government purchased Mare Island instead of Sausalito for its naval station."

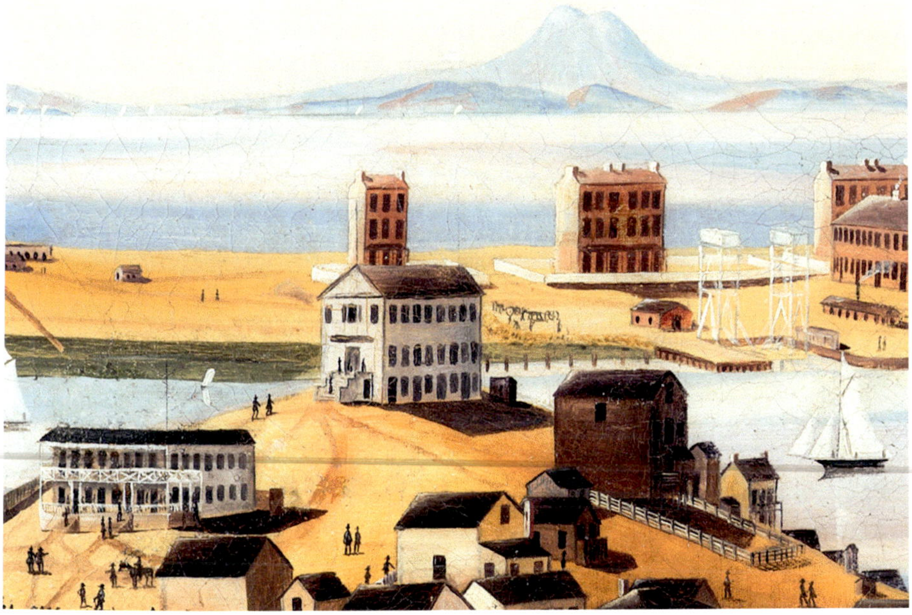

An 1857 oil painting depicts California's state capitol building atop York Street Hill in Vallejo. Lawmakers met here briefly in 1852 and 1853. The building was destroyed by fire in 1859. *[Vallejo Naval and Historical Museum]*

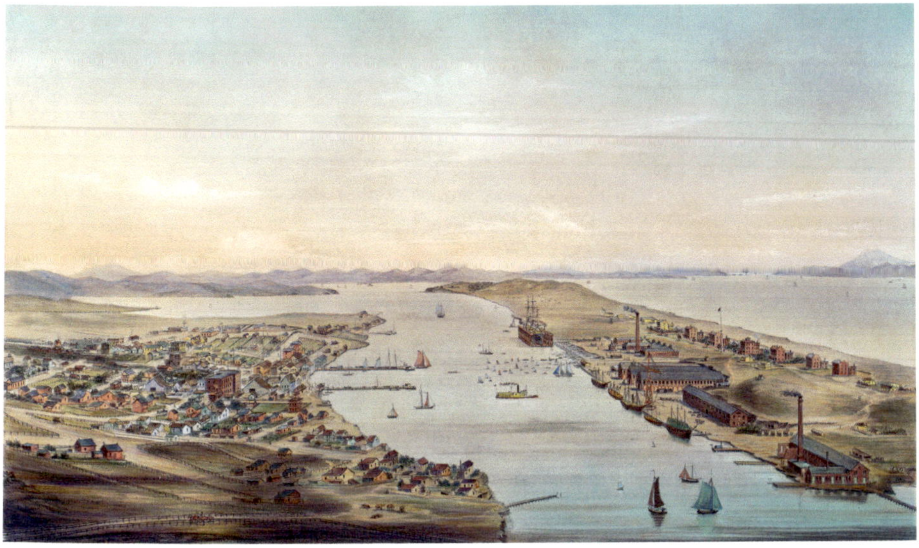

A birds-eye view of Vallejo on the left and Mare Island Naval Shipyard on the right, separated by the Mare Island Straight, c. 1860. *[Vallejo Naval and Historical Museum]*

Frisbie also had to defend the title to Gen. Vallejo's *Suscol* land grant, which included the Vallejo townsite, against bids by squatters to take the land from earlier settlers. "There was shooting; blood was spilled; murder was committed; the courts were filled with cases arising from this trouble," *Vallejo Chronicle* founder Frank Leach wrote in *Recollections of a Newspaper Man*. In his book, Leach described how a settler named Manuel Vera was accused of shooting and wounding a squatter. Vera was arrested and, since the town had no jail yet, was held temporarily in an apartment above Vallejo's post office in the Lower Georgia Street district. After dark, Leach wrote, a band of 100 or more squatters rode into town on horseback. While some held the horses, others found Vera and riddled him with bullets. Seventeen men were indicted for murder, but in the first case to come to trial "the jury brought in a verdict of 'not guilty,' so thereafter all the other cases were dismissed," Leach said.

The Navy's 1853 purchase of Mare Island and the 1854 opening of the first permanent Navy base on the West Coast set the future course for the city of Vallejo. It became a Navy town with plenty of ship-building and ship-repair jobs and a relatively stable economy that lasted until 1996, when Mare Island Naval Shipyard was finally closed along with many other military installations around the country.

2

The Navy Arrives, Vallejo's Future Course is Set

In 1850, two months after California entered the Union, Mare Island was reserved for military use by President Millard Fillmore. A survey in 1852 resulted in a recommendation that the island be turned into the first naval base on the West Coast, and the island was purchased for $83,491 on Jan. 4, 1853. Commander David Glasgow Farragut arrived at Mare Island on Sept. 16, 1854, ran off several squatters and took charge. With the Navy's arrival, Vallejo's future course was set. Farragut, later a Civil War hero, set about transforming a desolate site into a bustling Navy base capable of handling many types of ship repair work that until that time had been done by long-established East Coast Navy yards. After four years at Mare Island, he returned to sea duty and had a key role during the Civil War in capturing the port of New Orleans, in April 1862. Then he achieved a critical Union victory at the Battle of Mobile Bay in 1864, where he's remembered for saying, "Damn the torpedoes, full speed ahead!" That's close to what he actually said, which was, "Damn the torpedoes! Four bells! Capt. Drayton, go ahead! Jouett, full speed!"

The first naval vessel to be built on the West Coast, the USS *Saginaw*, was launched on March 3, 1859 at Mare Island. It was the first of more than 500 ships and submarines—nearly 400 during World War II alone—built at Mare Island over its 142-year history. Its World War I ships included the destroyer USS *Ward*, built in a record seventeen-and-a-half days. Seventeen nuclear submarines were constructed between the mid-1950s and 1970. Many other vessels underwent overhauls and repairs over the years. Other shipyard "firsts" included the only U.S. Navy super-dreadnought, the USS *California*, to be built on the West Coast (1916-1919); the Navy's first (1911) aircraft landing deck, a 157-foot-long wooden platform on the USS *Pennsylvania*; oldest (1857) ammunition depot on the West Coast; and the Navy's first interdenominational chapel, St. Peter's Chapel, dating to 1901.

As the shipyard grew, the city of Vallejo prospered, and Georgia Street, the town's main street, boomed with construction of new businesses, hotels and private residences. In

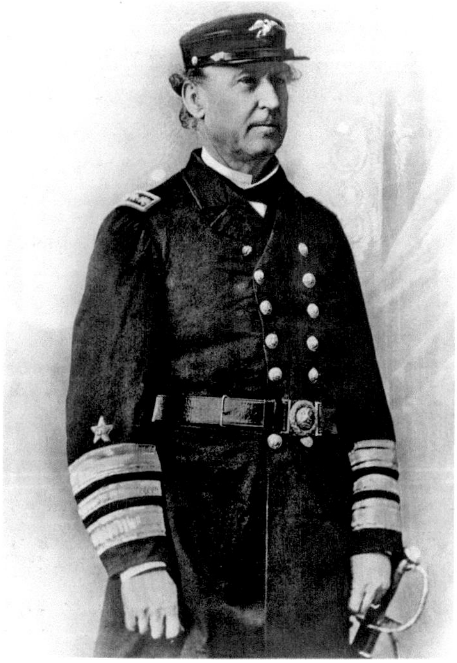

David Glasgow Farragut, the Navy's first admiral, established Mare Island Naval Shipyard in 1854. He won a critical Union victory at the 1864 Battle of Mobile Bay, where he gave his "Damn the torpedoes, full speed ahead" order. *[Vallejo Naval and Historical Museum]*

Images of America: Vallejo, author and historian Jim Kern says John Frisbie continued to promote the city, donating land for construction of a park, churches and a public school, and joining with other city leaders in founding Vallejo's first bank. Frisbie's first home was built on Georgia Street in 1856 across Sacramento Street from the first few blocks of Georgia Street's bustling commercial district, which years later gained notoriety as the "Strip," the "tenderloin," "Little Reno" and Vallejo's own "Barbary Coast." The Lower Georgia Street district included the first three blocks of Georgia Street, running eastward from the Napa River, and short stretches of the cross-streets of Branciforte, Santa Clara and Sacramento on either side of Georgia Street. The first few blocks of Virginia Street, one block to the north and running parallel to Georgia Street, were also in the district.

In an 1856 publication, *Sears' Pictorial Description of the United States*, Vallejo made a short list of "more prominent" California cities, along with San Francisco, Sacramento, San Jose, Monterey, Stockton, Benicia and San Diego. Los Angeles and Oakland didn't make the cut. Vallejo's boom continued through the Civil War years, and the ranks of military personnel at Mare Island grew with the assignment of a company of Marines to defend the shipyard in the event of attack by Confederate forces or sympathizers. The company, five officers and one hundred men, left by sea from New York in late 1862, only to be captured by the Confederates. Signing of a $261,000 ransom bond released the Marines' vessel. They reached Mare Island on Jan. 1, 1863. But in *A Long Line of Ships*, author

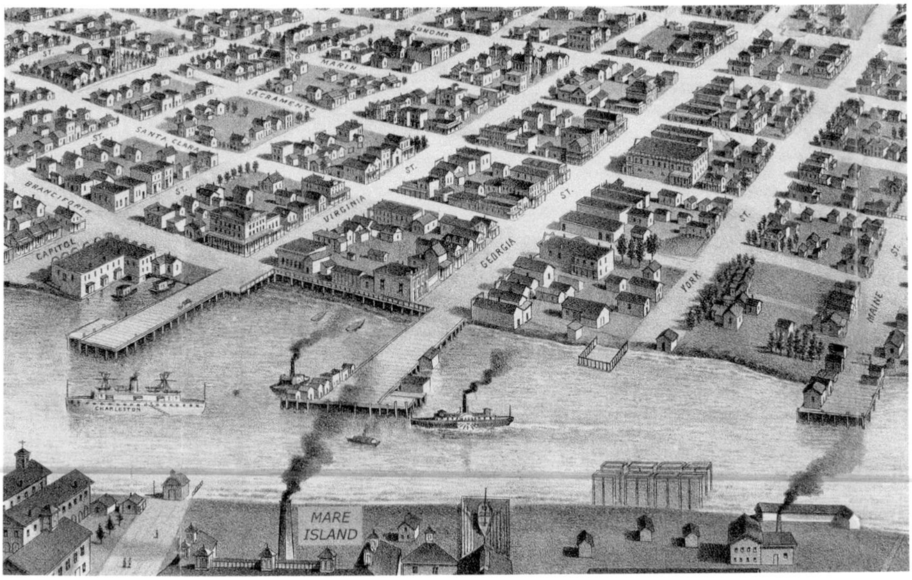

Nearly every block depicted in this early birds-eye view of Vallejo was leveled as part of the city's ambitious redevelopment project that began in the late 1950s. The last structure to be bulldozed was the Carnegie Library in 1970. *[Vallejo Naval and Historical Museum]*

Arnold S. Lott said the Marines, while they were a deterrent to any Rebel plans to seize Mare Island, "also created problems all their own which sometimes led the Commandant to feel it was almost as easy to get along without them as with them." Besides the Marines and sailors, in 1863 there were several hundred shipyard workers. During the war years and the post-Civil War years, sailors arrived on board American merchant ships as well as foreign ships from Russia, England, France, Japan, Italy and other countries.

By 1870 the shipyard that had started with a dozen men had grown into an important shipbuilding and repair yard, with about 1,500 workers, a hospital, ordnance magazine and Marine barracks. Also by 1870, Vallejo was the deep-water port and rail terminus for several counties and much of the Sacramento Valley. A. D. Starr had built a large flour mill in South Vallejo, and large, profitable lumber yards had been established. Vallejo's first bank, headed by Daniel Webster Harrier, opened in 1867, followed by a second bank, managed by John Frisbie, in 1870. "It was an era of prosperity, and everybody engaged in business was making money," Frank Leach wrote in *Recollections of a Newspaper Man.*

However, after the Civil War, the number of Navy ships shrank dramatically. A fleet that in 1866 had numbered almost 700 ships was cut to 185 within a few years. By the end of 1876 the Mare Island shipyard work force averaged only 330 men. But many laid-off shipyard workers were able to find jobs at private ship repair and construction yards that were developing on the Vallejo side of the Napa River, now called Mare Island Strait.

Many of the estimated 600 scow schooners that hauled cargo on San Francisco Bay and inland waters were built at the Vallejo yards. They also built tugs, sloops, barges and even a Navy monitor. When a proposal for a Vallejo-side cooperative shipbuilding association surfaced in 1874, the idea was hailed by the *San Francisco Bulletin*, which editorialized that Vallejo "offers greater facilities for this business than any other place on the Pacific Coast. The trouble with Vallejo has long been that the people trust too much to the Navy Yard, when that institution should be an incident to the prosperity of the city." Prophetic words, given the decision that led to the 1996 closure of Mare Island and the loss of Vallejo's major employer.

By the early 1870s, the Navy's first prison had been built on Mare Island. Author Rodney Watterson, in *Whips to Walls: Naval Discipline from Flogging to Progressive-Era Reform at Portsmouth Prison,* said a naval prison system was needed because Congress had banned flogging in 1850, even though veteran Navy officers argued flogging was the best way to deal with crews "highly populated by ruffians, thugs, and foreigners." Watterson also quoted from an 1885 report by Navy Commander N. H. Farquhar, who said, "The dregs of all countries seem to get into our service," and "only those remain in the Navy who cannot better themselves elsewhere." Farquhar, in pressing for higher-caliber recruits, added the Navy sailor had a history of being an illiterate "good-for-nothing fellow" and "a drunkard, and the victim of pimps, runners and prostitutes."

Sailors who met Farquhar's description fit right in at some of the saloons and card rooms in Vallejo. In one high-stakes draw poker game, described in a lengthy article that ran in newspapers around the country, two gamblers got into an argument in 1867 over a big poker pot. Lou Prindley claimed that under West Coast poker rules his full house beat the other gambler's straight flush. The other man, a ship engineer from the East Coast, argued that his hand was the winner under the rules he played by. The article stated that the engineer grabbed Prindley and gouged out his right eye, and Prindley then pulled out a long knife and killed the other man. Prindley fled from Vallejo to Arizona, where he ran a Faro game and was known as "One-eyed Lou."

Fatal disputes in the Lower Georgia district involved more than gambling. A *Vallejo Weekly Chronicle* article described an Aug. 21, 1867, dispute over the Metropolitan Hotel's utility bill that ended with the shooting of the new Vallejo Gas Light Company's superintendent, M. P. Young. Young walked a few blocks from the gas company to the hotel, at the corner of Virginia and Santa Clara streets in the Lower Georgia district, where he accused one of the owners, John H. Lee, a pioneer Vallejoan, of fashioning a bypass around his gas meter to keep his bill down. Lee drew a pistol and fired two shots at Young, who died a month later from his injuries. If there were charges filed, the newspaper made no record of it.

Arsonists, possibly disgruntled volunteer firefighters who had been replaced by a new company of volunteers, began setting fires around town in mid-1876. Leaders of the new company received anonymous death threats, warning them to not respond to fire alarms. A "vigilance committee" started night patrols but stopped after the arson incidents ceased. But the arsonists struck again at about 3 a.m. on a Sunday, torching the new company's firehouse. The blaze destroyed the firehouse, located in the Lower Georgia district on Virginia Street, and all the equipment inside. A trail of dripped coal oil was noticed at daybreak, leading from a saloon frequented by some of the former volunteers to the firehouse. "No one was arrested for the deed, though nearly everybody was satisfied as to who was responsible for it," Frank Leach wrote in *Recollections of a Newspaper Man.* New equipment was purchased and kept under guard at a new location. "Whether the vandals became frightened, or were satisfied with the destruction of the old apparatus we never knew. We had no more trouble," said Leach.

Violence could occur anywhere, even at political gatherings. At a downtown Democratic meeting, two men got into a fight over comments by a speaker, and one was stabbed. The Sept. 4, 1869, *Vallejo Weekly Chronicle* said the knifer, John Morgan, had to be hustled off to the county jail because of concern that "an effort would be made to take Morgan out of the hands of the officer and lynch him, as a large crowd followed, crying, 'Lynch him! Hang him!' and other frenzied expressions of like import."

Business owners along Georgia and Virginia streets had to deal with counterfeiters trying to pass off fake $1 coins as real silver dollars, according to a Nov. 15, 1880, *Vallejo Evening Chronicle* story. The town constable arrested Al Bowles and Ben Nickles and found a sack of a few hundred dollar pieces, along with chemicals and electro-plating equipment. Bowles had spent an entire day making small purchases at a bakery, saloon, cigar stand, jeweler, two restaurants, a clothing store and other shops, handing over the bogus coins and getting change back. Another accomplice, Tom Kennedy, was arrested in San Francisco. He was believed to be the ringleader.

Opium was another concern in the Lower Georgia Street district, according to an 1887 editorial in the *Vallejo Evening Chronicle.* The editorial described how the "opium fiends" had spread to outlying areas of the town, but added, "We have it on undoubted authority that there is an opium den in the principal part of our city, kept by white people. It is frequented chiefly by boys, some of them sons of Georgia street merchants." The editorial went on to say that "until within the last year or two in Vallejo, opium smoking was confined entirely, we might say, to Chinese dens, where disreputable characters congregated and indulged their depraved appetites. But the evil circle has been constantly widening, and now 'opium lay-outs' are to be found in various parts of town and the number of victims has increased in a like ratio." Later news accounts said the opium-den operators were "scattered to the winds," but opium use was reported in the Dec. 5, 1895, *Evening Chronicle* in two houses on the edge of the Lower Georgia district. The report described a city order that the tenants vacate the premises. "The Chinese opium joints and Japanese rendezvous must go to the suburbs," the *Evening Chronicle* said, adding that city trustees demanded that future tenants "comply with the ordinary and accepted rules observed by law-abiding citizens who have a due regard both for the laws of proper sanitation and good government."

The Navy cutbacks that had reduced the Mare Island workforce during the mid-1870s gradually eased, and by the 1890s, shipyard employment had grown to about 900 men. That was the count when a mysterious explosion sank the USS *Maine* in Havana Harbor on Feb. 15, 1898. That led to the presidential declaration on April 25 that started the Spanish-American War. At that point more than 1,700 workers were rushing to complete repairs on several ships. And during that same period there were numerous accounts of violent crime involving Navy sailors, Marines and others in the Lower Georgia Street district.

A Jan. 28, 1890 newspaper report told of the fatal shooting of John Ryan, a seaman stationed on the USS *Independence*, in the Philadelphia House, a 116 Georgia St. saloon. The barkeeper, Theodore Donguli, was charged with second-degree murder and was eventually sentenced to eleven years in state prison. The *Vallejo Evening Chronicle* said some drunken sailors started kicking in the door of the saloon and Donguli came out and fired one shot, hitting Ryan. "There were at least a dozen drunken sailors rolling and struggling about in the crowd, and this had been the condition of affairs all afternoon," the *Evening Chronicle* said. "The people of this city should demand that some relief be afforded them against the continuance of a locality in the very doorway of the place, where such things can go on without interruption. Donguli is credited with keeping as orderly a place as dance-halls can be, but still a sailor was slashed up in his front hall a few weeks ago and now a man is shot out of his very doors. There is no possible peace and order where liquor has full sway with no restraint."

Sidewalks as well as barrooms were crime scenes. On March 28, 1890, the *Vallejo Evening Chronicle* reported that Maurice O'Callaghan, informed that a couple of Marines planned to beat him, "armed himself with a revolver and late in the afternoon met them in front of Brown's butcher shop on Georgia street." Attacked, O'Callaghan shot at both men, missing one but giving Marine Cpl. Patrick Moylan "a slight wound along his left temple." The city attorney, Lewis G. Harrier, wanted O'Callaghan tried for assault with intent to kill, but the newspaper said O'Callaghan's lawyer, F. W. Hall, "was able to make out a case of self-defense," and Justice of the Peace George Demmon dismissed the charge.

A few years later, the *San Francisco Call* said the Solano County Grand Jury's report for 1893 singled out Vallejo officials for "the lax manner in which the township officials perform their duty with regard to gambling, houses of prostitution, etc." In June 7 and June 16, 1893, accounts, the *Call* said the jury heard testimony from police officers that despite repeated appeals to remove houses of ill repute from Vallejo "the city officials had denied the police proper support." Jurors, learning that no city or county taxes were being paid by brothel operators, ordered that the taxes be collected immediately. The *Call* also said county supervisors were accused of "gross carelessness and laxity in the discharge of their duty," adding that the officials were "trembling with fear" and trying to suppress the Grand Jury document. In another 1893 story, the *Call* said Vallejo authorities were cracking down on minors entering saloons and "all gambling games are also to be suppressed." A June 8, 1894, report in the *Vallejo Evening Chronicle* said burglaries, muggings and other crimes got bad enough that a five-man Pinkerton Protective Patrol was being set up in the downtown area and adjacent residential streets. "Of late, it has been almost a daily occurrence to hear of someone being sand-bagged or garroted, or worse still, to be cruelly beaten," the *Evening Chronicle* said. "Some people blame our police, but they are a wide-awake body of men. This remark calls to mind the old saying, 'One cat cannot watch twenty mice.'"

Heavy drinking was enough of a problem, excluding any criminal activity. The *San Francisco Chronicle* filed a Dec. 22, 1894, report about a fire that destroyed the Philadelphia House, where seaman John Ryan had been killed nearly five years earlier. The fire, in what the *Chronicle* described as "a sort of low-class sailors' lodging-house," burned to death the owner, Jack Finn, and two other men. The location "was the scene of many carousals, a particularly big one occurring on the night of the fire," the *Chronicle* said. "While the revelers were lying drunk the building, by some means, took fire, and burning rapidly prevented their rescue, if indeed anyone knew of their being there. Their blackened corpses were found next morning in the ruins." The newspaper added that the boarding house "has been the scene of many disgraceful affairs, so that little regret is felt at its destruction." A new Philadelphia House was built the following year.

The *Vallejo Evening Chronicle* reported on Dec. 2, 1895, that city trustees called for a four-month hiatus on new liquor licenses. "Vallejo contains about 75 places where liquor is sold or one to every 100 inhabitants, not 100 men but 100 men, women and children," the newspaper said. "This is a truly startling state of affairs and calls for action by the authority which has the control of the sale of liquor." The article concluded by saying the number of saloons should be reduced "to a ratio with the number of inhabitants which will not be startling to our own citizens and absolutely terrifying to strangers."

Where there was drinking and gambling, there also was prostitution. A Dec. 9, 1895, *Vallejo Evening Chronicle* article reported the gunshot slaying of one Hattie Allen, a prostitute in a "disorderly house" in Vallejo. "She was killed at the moment a rift seemed to be opening in the clouds, bringing to her mind a brighter view and happy prospects," the article stated. "The slayer had promised to marry her and take her to scenes where her past life would be unknown, and where she might redeem herself in leading a decent life." The shooter was identified as William Stanton, a Marine Corps private who tried to kill himself but recovered. The *San Francisco Chronicle* reported Feb. 28, 1896, on the search for "Tillie Hill, the procuress," wanted for luring two girls into a Vallejo brothel after they responded to an ad for restaurant work. Authorities also ordered a closure of the brothel, which "will certainly result in the windup of one of the most disreputable places that ever existed in Vallejo," the article stated.

In 1896, three Vallejo newspapers, the *Times, Chronicle* and *News,* launched a crusade against gambling in Georgia Street saloons. "Vallejo is becoming the Monte Carlo of California," the *Times* declared. "Gambling hells are doing business openly on Georgia Street in violation of the State law, debauching our youths and injuring the business and fair name of this town." In praising the crusade, which resulted in a shutdown of the gambling, the *San Francisco Call* said the papers showed that reforms are possible "if only the editors of any locality combine to accomplish it."

The *San Francisco Chronicle* also had a Sept. 3, 1896, report about a police night watchman, Frank Toal, being shot and killed by a drunken friend, Dan Wynne, in front of the Castle saloon on Lower Georgia Street. Toal, in his third year as a city watchman, fired back, wounding Wynne, who died a day later. Wynne had been arguing with other saloon patrons mainly about a rowboat ferry he operated between Vallejo and Mare Island. Wynne was "a good man when sober, but a veritable demon when in liquor," the article stated. Another article the same day, in the *Santa Cruz Evening Sentinel,* described Wynne as "crazy when intoxicated," and Toal as "a good officer, but without judgment."

A Feb. 5, 1897, story in the *San Francisco Call* described a late-night incident on Georgia Street involving a man who was "at the point of a pistol ordered to dance a jig. Upon hesitating three pistol shots were fired in the air over his head, with a warning that the next shot would go through him if he did not comply with the demand of the young sport holding the weapon. The dance commenced and was kept up until a crowd began to gather, when the young ruffian slipped away."

A Dec. 19, 1898, account in the *Vallejo Evening Chronicle* described a drunken brawl between a Marine private and Joe Curran, proprietor of Old Ketchum's on Lower Georgia Street. The article stated that an argument over a dice game ended with Curran using a pistol to first hammer and then shoot at the Marine, who in turn grabbed a pipe and began hitting Curran. The two men "were doing their best each to hammer the other into insensibility," the *Evening Chronicle* said. "Curran used the butt end of a revolver, and the marine says he used the business end once, the bullet grazing his cheek. Curran claims the marine wielded a lead pipe. His many bruises and contusions back up his assertion. The marine's teeth also closed on Curran's arm making a nasty wound."

As the 19th Century drew to a close, a pattern that would repeat itself time and again was obvious: Problems in the Lower Georgia Street district would slowly escalate, to the point that authorities, usually backed by newspaper editors, would take action. Under pressure, properties that were the most trouble would calm down for a time. But before long criminal activity would start again.

A New Century Opens, Crime Patterns Persist

The seriousness of Vallejo's crime problems was described by retired Superior Court Judge Joseph M. Raines in a 1957 *Vallejo Times-Herald* column. Raines recalled that when he was a district attorney in the early 1900s, homicides occurred in the lower blocks and waterfront at a rate of eight to ten a month. "But seldom was there anyone to prosecute for the simple reason that the principals either were dead or unknown," *Vallejo Times-Herald* Managing Editor Wyman Riley wrote in the column. "Bodies in the channel were not uncommon and even with the casual treatment accorded crimes of violence by early-day newspapers, it is readily apparent from old files that Vallejo never has had anything to match the crime that occurred just before and just after the turn of the century."

The 20th Century had barely opened when, on Jan. 3, 1900, the *San Francisco Chronicle* reported that a trusted steward on the USS *Hartford* had deserted, leaving behind a large number of debts to his shipmates and several hundred dollars of unpaid bills in Vallejo. Tsu Hirokowa, the paper reported, had "developed a real touch of American sporting blood" and had lost large sums gambling in the Lower Georgia Street clubs. "One line of sport led Hirokowa to another until he had painted the Vallejo tenderloin a brilliant hue," the *Chronicle* said.

The *Vallejo Evening Chronicle* reported on Sept. 29, 1900, that the Pearl Saloon in the Lower Georgia district was "the scene of great excitement." A drunken ex-Marine, David Barker, drew a pistol and started firing, irate over practical jokes played on him by others in the saloon. He missed the bartender, William "Yank" Savage, but proprietor Frank Burns and patron James Coakley were wounded. Coakley, a shipyard worker, "happened to be half asleep in a chair, and was the last man in the room to realize the danger about him," the *Evening Chronicle* said. The report added that Barker was "drunk enough to be foolish. At one time he would have his pockets filled with water through a funnel, another time his hat was saturated with alcohol, replaced on his head and later set on fire. These were funny things, the crowd would laugh, and Barker's indignation only added to their amusement."

Also in 1900, the state Supreme Court rejected an appeal filed by J. T. Murphy, who had been convicted in Vallejo of "playing the game of keno." The unanimous March 10, 1900, decision upheld a city ordinance that prohibited "the playing of specified games of chance, and all banking and percentage games." Murphy argued the city ordinance didn't specify that keno was a percentage game, but the high court held that the city could prohibit all games of chance, whether or not specified by name. The ruling was seen as a classic case supporting the right of California cities to be more restrictive in their ordinances than state laws, providing the state hadn't taken jurisdiction in a particular area. The decision had an impact on the Lower Georgia Street district because of the various games of chance that could be found there, and helped William Stanford, a shipyard mechanic with no police experience, who in April 1900 was named Vallejo's first police chief. Stanford, who served as police chief until 1936, promptly began targeting the gamblers.

Among the saloons that Stanford watched closely was the Waldorf, located on the corner of Georgia and Marin streets, in the center of Vallejo's expanding business district and one block east of the main saloon district. Stanford's focus on the Waldorf quickly put him at odds with the proprietor, W. R. Acock, who told the chief to stay out of his bar. In late September, Stanford was just across the street when told that trouble was brewing at the Waldorf and there might be gunplay. But when he tried to enter the saloon, Acock stopped him and then hit him on the head with the butt of his pistol. The *Vallejo Evening Chronicle* reported on Sept. 29, 1900, that Acock told the police chief to leave, adding, "As Acock spoke these words he reached over with his left hand apparently to lay a stump of a cigar on a slot machine, but in reality to take out his gun with the right hand, unobserved by the Chief. Then with his left he grabbed the Chief and struck him on the head a vicious blow that laid the scalp open, following it up with other blows, dazing the Chief." Stanford pulled out his gun and fired, but was blinded by blood from his head wound and missed Acock. Onlookers grabbed both men to prevent any more shooting, and Acock was jailed on a charge of assaulting an officer. On Oct. 12, the *San Francisco Call* reported that Acock got a clever lawyer who got the charge dismissed on a technicality. Stanford and District Attorney Frank Devlin then filed a new charge against Acock, who wound up paying a $200 fine. Acock in turn filed two criminal complaints and one civil complaint against Stanford, but those complaints eventually were dismissed. He also proposed to have the city charter revised to eliminate the new police department, but that proposal went nowhere. The *Call* also reported on Oct. 25 that Vallejo Mayor Joel A. Harvey vetoed as unconstitutional a city ordinance giving Stanford clear-cut authority to regulate retail liquor sales and to prevent certain games in places where liquor is sold. "The mayor claims that the ordinance is unconstitutional, on the ground that it is repugnant to the constitution of the United States and that of the State and the provisions of the (city) charter," the *Call* said.

Despite the challenges and outright opposition from Acock and others that he faced, Stanford didn't abandon his clean-up crusade. The Dec. 29, 1900, *Vallejo Evening Chronicle* reported that Stanford focused on the Leader Saloon, located at 225 Georgia St., getting warrants that accused 31 people of playing craps, Klondyke, poker, keno and card games. The police chief also investigated the Waldorf, but the *Evening Chronicle* said gamblers there had been tipped off by Solano County Sheriff George Savage and "many of them took the train for San Francisco" to avoid arrest. While no arrests for gambling were made at the Waldorf, the relentless chief several days later filed a complaint accusing Acock of selling liquor without a license at the place.

"The reign of the gambling element in Vallejo seems likely to come to an abrupt conclusion," the *Evening Chronicle* said, adding, "Should gambling be stamped out in our city, the praise will belong to our Chief of Police, and not to the officer whose duty it was to move in this matter as Sheriff of the county. Sheriff Savage, whose unwillingness to interfere in the open state of things in this city, has been very marked."

An "abrupt conclusion" of gambling wasn't in the cards. In 1904, authorities in Vallejo and elsewhere in Solano County began cracking down on slot machines, which had been outlawed by the state Legislature, and on poker games. There were 112 known slot machines in Vallejo, each subject to a $10 quarterly license fee or about $4,500 a year. "This was considerable revenue that will have to be made up in some other way," the *San Francisco Chronicle* said in an Oct. 2, 1904, report, adding that state law required the shutdown of slots and Solano County "is one of the last in California to enforce it."

Besides the arrests and prosecutions of lawbreakers, there were efforts to create other activities and places where sailors could gather, without the drinking, gambling and prostitution found in and around many saloons. In 1902, a major fund-raising effort was launched for a Vallejo clubhouse for sailors. The *Los Angeles Times* said the goal was to provide the sailors with "comfortable quarters and wholesome pastime while on shore, instead of being obliged to resort to cheap boarding-houses, saloons and other immoral places for food, shelter and recreation." In 1903, President Theodore Roosevelt laid the cornerstone for the Naval YMCA, built at a cost of $62,000. Its location, on the corner of Santa Clara and York streets, was one short block away from the heart of the Lower Georgia Street district.

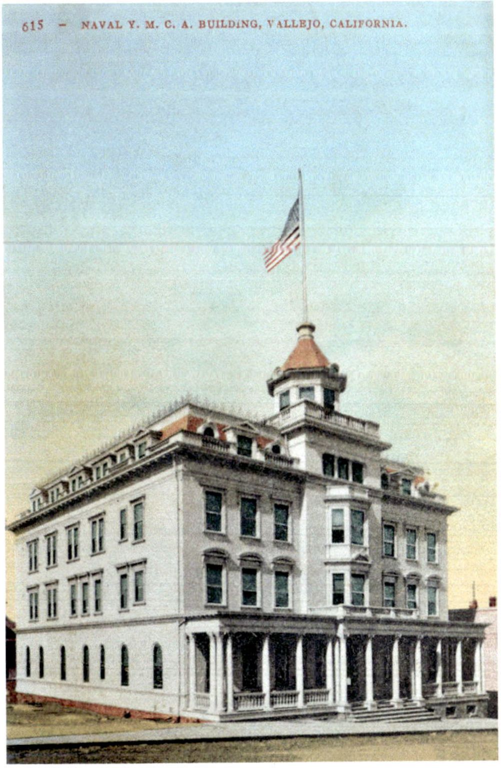

The Naval YMCA, located a block away from the Lower Georgia district, is displayed in this early-1900s postcard. *[Vallejo Naval and Historical Museum]*

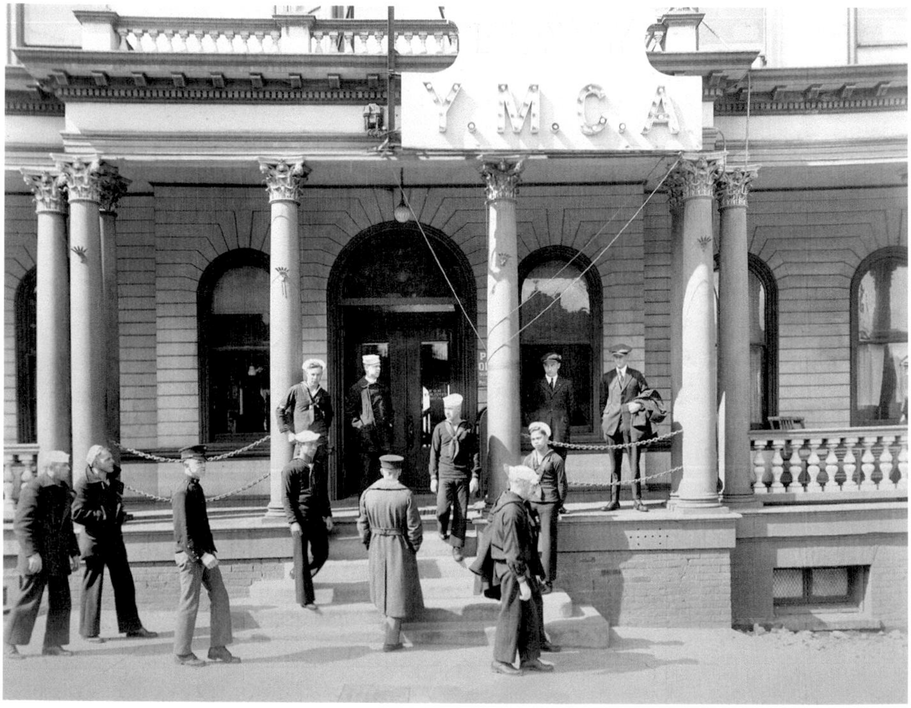

Sailors and Marines in front of the Naval YMCA. *[Vallejo Naval and Historical Museum]*

The Debate Over Vallejo's Saloon Count

The extent of the saloon trade in Vallejo was revealed in an April 7, 1905, *San Francisco Call* story about Vallejo officials granting 86 liquor licenses to saloon-keepers, in a town of only about 8,000 residents. The licenses had been held up mainly as a result of the continuing "war" between Acock and Stanford. Acock had run the Waldorf as a gambling house when Vallejo was an open town, and since the closing of the games in 1904 Stanford had been trying to make sure that gambling didn't start up again, the *Call* said. Acock finally got his liquor license after promising to keep poker games out of his saloon.

Stanford was at it again in 1906, informing the saloon-keepers in the Lower Georgia Street "tenderloin" that they could no longer just pay a fine equal to the liquor license fee in order to sell booze. "It is also ordered that there must be no more music in the tenderloin," the *San Francisco Chronicle* said in a story headlined, "Vallejo Issues Morality Orders."

A Sept. 26, 1906, report in the *Washington Post* stated that reformer Forbes H. Brown, a shipyard clerk, traveled to the nation's capital city to meet with Navy Secretary Charles Bonaparte and argue that "immorality exists in his home city which is frequented largely by sailors from Mare Island." Brown contended that Vallejo had 150 low-class saloons "besides many gambling places and other disreputable houses," the *Post* said. A month later, the *San Francisco Call* reported that Brown's claims were challenged by Vallejo Mayor J. J. Madigan, who said there were 92 saloons and the town's population was 16,000. Even accepting Madigan's figures, Bonaparte termed the proportion of saloons to residents "alarmingly and wholly unnecessarily high. It amounts to one saloon for less than each 140 inhabitants." Bonaparte and the Mare Island commandant, Rear Adm. H. W. Lyon, threatened to have the Navy's work done elsewhere. Madigan, fearing the loss of shipyard jobs, then gave in and agreed to reduce the number of saloons.

The Navy secretary said the saloon total should be 46, and "that persons convicted of crime or notoriously bad or keepers of brothels or gambling houses be not permitted to sell liquor and that saloons be closed on Sundays and holidays," the *San Francisco Call* reported.

The battle over vice heated up again in August 1910, with Police Chief Stanford and a new mayor, J. F. Chappell, being summoned before a grand jury to discuss complaints that liquor was being sold "in the tenderloin dance halls, that gambling flourished and that all kinds of violations of the law were being countenanced," the *Call* reported. In some cases, "working girls" were renting rooms above downtown stores. After spending an hour with Chappell and Stanford, according to the Aug. 8, 1910, *Vallejo Evening Chronicle*, "the Grand Jury informed them that they would leave the matter in their hands." Two weeks

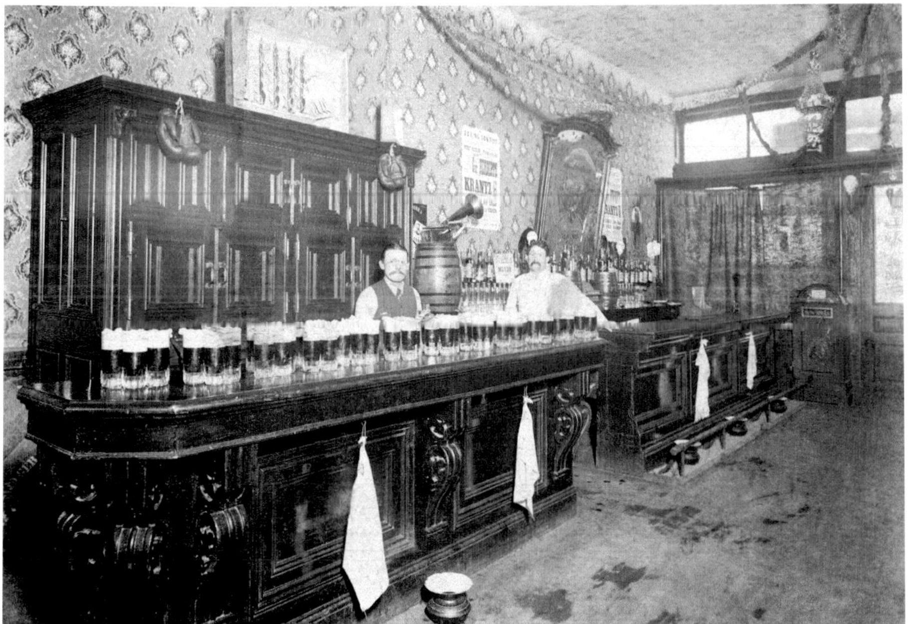

In this 1903 photo, Eugene Williams, right, was ready for a ferryboat load of sailors or shipyard workers, or both, at his bar in the Lower Georgia Street district. *[Vallejo Naval and Historical Museum]*

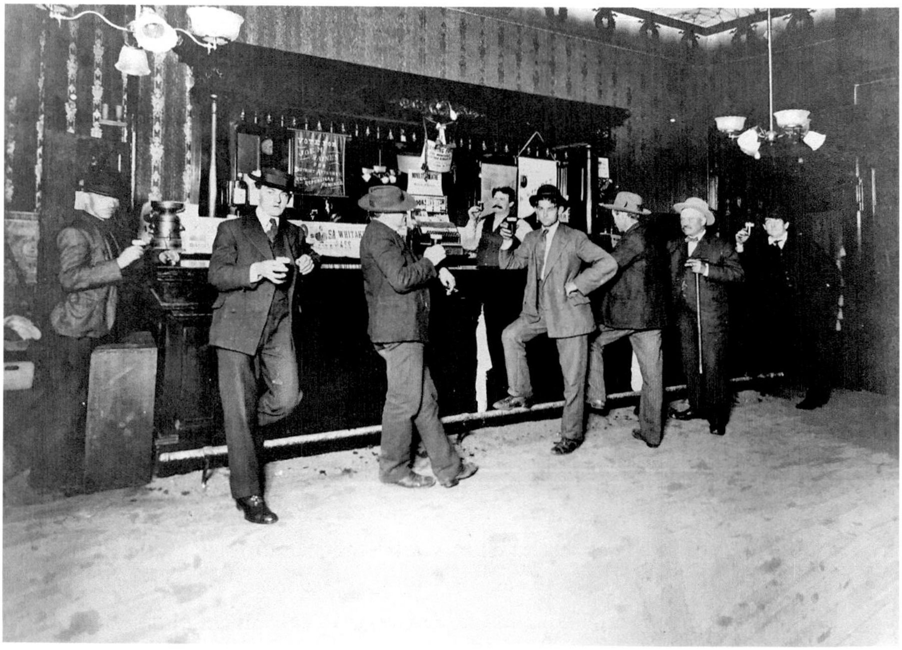

Patrons gather for drinks at the Monticello Bar and Athletic Club, 115 Georgia St., in 1905. During World War II, it was the Palm Grill, and the liquor was still flowing. *[Vallejo Naval and Historical Museum]*

later, the paper reported that the city attorney, William O'Donnell, had been authorized to hire special counsel to help in prosecuting cases of illegal liquor sales. But the trustees balked at a plan to require saloons to install 18-by-30-inch or larger glass panes on their doors "through which passers-by may see who is frequenting the interiors of local thirst emporiums," the *Chronicle* said.

On Sept. 22, 1910, the *Vallejo Evening Chronicle* also reported that a proposal to increase the number of saloon licenses was rejected by city trustees, under pressure from Adm. Hugo Osterhaus who had taken over as shipyard commandant earlier in the year. The *Los Angeles Herald* version of the same story said Osterhaus stated "that he had no disposition to interfere with the municipal affairs of Vallejo, but he must protect the enlisted men coming here and would feel it to be his duty to recommend to the navy department that the number of ships sent to Mare Island be reduced to the minimum if the additional liquor licenses were granted."

A busy 1910 wound down with city trustees deciding to permit no new saloons in the two lower blocks of Georgia Street, the *San Francisco Call* reported on Dec. 21. The *Call* noted that the suggestion came from Adm. Osterhaus. The suggestion was a heavy-handed one—the Navy was continuing to threaten that the number of ships coming to Mare Island would be reduced unless conditions improved in Vallejo. The city also decided to impose penalties, including license revocations, for any saloons that sold liquor "to an intoxicated man, a minor, or a woman," the *Vallejo Daily Times* reported on July 18, 1913.

What did sailors have to say about all the clean-up efforts? One, Don Ray, a sailor serving aboard the USS *West Virginia*, said in a letter published in *Our Navy* magazine in 1910 that sailors and Marines on liberty were being harassed by police. Ray added that police were ignoring Vallejoans acting up as much as the servicemen. Chief Stanford denied the claims made by Ray, who had focused on the 4th of July celebration in Vallejo that year.

"Of course, some of us got drunk and raised a little disturbance," Ray said. "That's what pay days and saloons are for, but I can't see that this one-horse village, which can't even boast a town pump, has any more dignity to sustain than the cities of the east and west coast, where enlisted men are better treated in every way." Ray added, "If we are such a bad lot as these sensitive citizens think, it is strange that we are treated so well in other cities along the coast, especially San Francisco and Oakland." City police would be "doping off" when locals were throwing firecrackers and "dashing talcum powder and confetti in the faces of anyone," Ray wrote. "But if an enlisted man grew hilarious with patriotism, etc., the policemen would suddenly come out of their dope and make a few arrests."

Confrontations between authorities and operators of saloons, gambling houses and brothels in the Lower Georgia Street district often didn't amount to much more than what Ray described as sailors growing "hilarious with patriotism." But when a deputy sheriff shot and killed a Marine private in a downtown club on June 8, 1912, an angry mob tried to lynch the officer. Armed Marines rushed from Mare Island to Vallejo to protect Deputy Sheriff Frank Meyer from hundreds of sailors and Marines following Meyer's slaying of Joseph Workman in the Waldorf Annex. An *Oakland Tribune* report said Workman was ordered to leave the gambling club but instead started fighting with Meyer, who knocked him down. Workman's friends surrounded the officer, who then hit the Marine with a blackjack and shot him. Meyer was taken to the nearby city jail, followed by the mob. "There were loud threats of lynching, and the police, fearing their inability to resist an attack on the jail, hurriedly summoned aid from Mare Island," the *Tribune* said. The carbine-toting Marines forced the sailors and Marines down to the waterfront, where they were ordered to get into launches that took them back to the shipyard.

The shooting and near-lynching of Meyer led to a public vote against gambling in Vallejo, and local police began conducting more raids to stop the activity—not always with success. A June 21, 1913, *Vallejo Daily Times* account described how William Tobin and Charles McCauley, brother of the city's public works commissioner, were arrested at the Exile Club in the Lower Georgia district by an officer who stated he saw the men "playing cards, and exchange money and chips on the table." The case went to trial, but after fifteen minutes of deliberation, jurors found the men innocent. That followed testimony by McCauley, Tobin and two others that they were playing pinochle, not poker, and that the three dollars the officer took from the table wasn't betting money. But six men nabbed in a raid on the

Philadelphia House, 114 Georgia, two months later didn't get off so easily. The newspaper reported on Aug. 19, 1913, that they were "caught absolutely red-handed at that most horrible game of black jack" and "evidence in the way of cards, money and even a watch which had been staked was secured." They all pleaded guilty and were fined $20 apiece.

The newspaper's Aug. 13, 1913, edition carried a story about a fired special police officer, Leroy Alvord, complaining that he was dismissed because of pressure from William Carruthers, following several raids by Alvord on dice games at Carruthers' "resort in the tenderloin." Alvord said he had been "between two fires continually, from the police department for not making arrests and from those who pay me my salary, for making them." Police Chief Stanford declined to comment, while the city's commissioner of public health and safety, William Blake, said, "The charge that Carruthers wielded any influence is absurd." Blake said he had found no record of arrests, was getting complaints about the gambling, and decided that matters "should be handled differently." The same Aug. 13, 1913, edition described the trial of Hong Sam on an opium possession charge filed following a raid on his place near the Lower Georgia district. He was fined the minimum $100 at the conclusion of police court proceedings, which had been postponed seven times. Sam insisted that he didn't know the opium was in his house, but an opium "outfit" was found under a trap door and "it appeared from the evidence introduced that he had been in the habit of renting the outfit to various Chinese," the *Times* stated.

Such "Wild West" situations occurred even as major civic improvements were being made. Vallejo's downtown streets were being paved and sidewalks were being improved, ferry service to San Francisco had expanded, new downtown street lights were installed, and a new library, city hall, hospital, high school, the Empress Theater and several new churches were built or were in the planning stages. "Vallejo has been renamed," the *San Francisco Call* reported in April 26, 1908, adding that unofficially "it is popularly known as 'The City of Cash.'" The *Call* said the annual payroll to workers living in Vallejo, mainly from the Navy shipyard, topped $2 million a year, adding, "This cash speaks for itself; it speaks, too, of the chances that lie within the limits of Vallejo for the man who can foresee the future. Vallejo has always been a city of possibilities, but these possibilities have become actual facts in the last few years." Despite all the progress, the waterfront and the first few blocks of Georgia Street remained the usual problem areas, even though saloons shared those same blocks with grocery, department and drug stores, butcher shops, a fruit and vegetable stand and other shops.

The Lower Georgia district wasn't the only trouble spot. The Vallejo Pavilion, a skating rink that doubled as the hub for many civic events over the years, was the scene of a free-for-all involving about 100 sailors and civilians. The half-hour fight at the Pavilion, three blocks from the Lower Georgia district, started when a drunken sailor bumped into other skaters. "Women screamed, and red-blooded enlisted men and civilians with the battle lust gleaming in their eyes waded into the hostilities," the *Vallejo Evening Chronicle* reported on June 16, 1913. "Some gore was spilled, some eyes were discolored and perhaps a few women fainted."

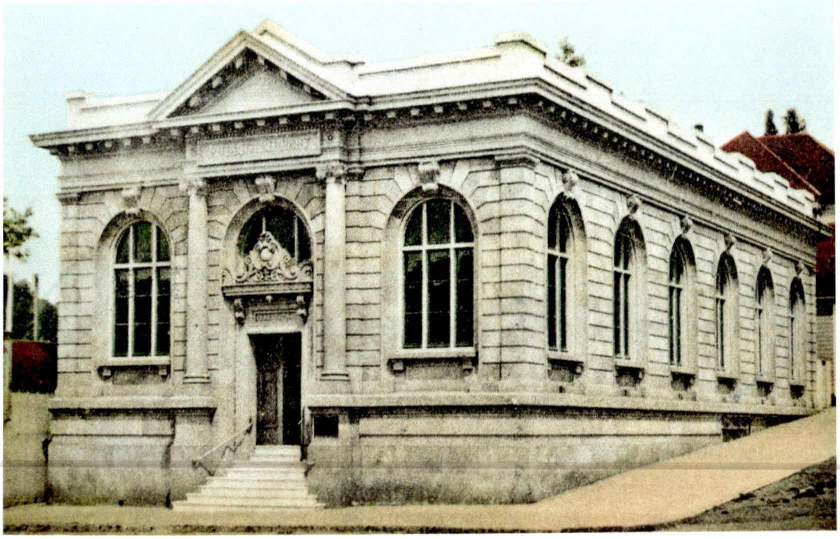

Industrialist Andrew Carnegie donated money for libraries in communities across the United States. That included $20,000 for Vallejo's Carnegie Library, dedicated on July 4, 1904. *[Vallejo Naval and Historical Museum]*

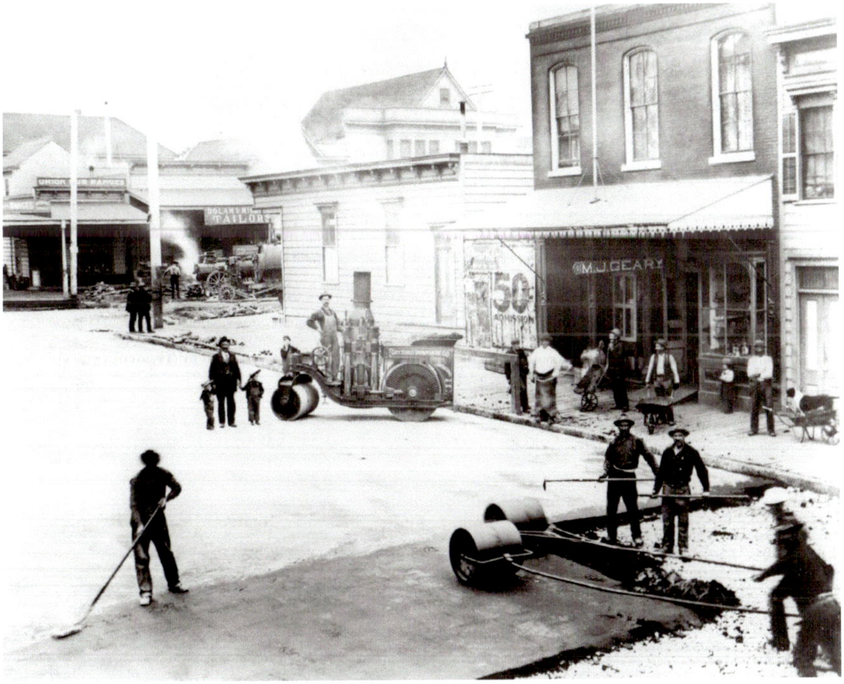

Workers began paving Lower Georgia Street in about 1912. Paved streets were among many civic improvements as Vallejo entered the 20th Century. *[Vallejo Naval and Historical Museum]*

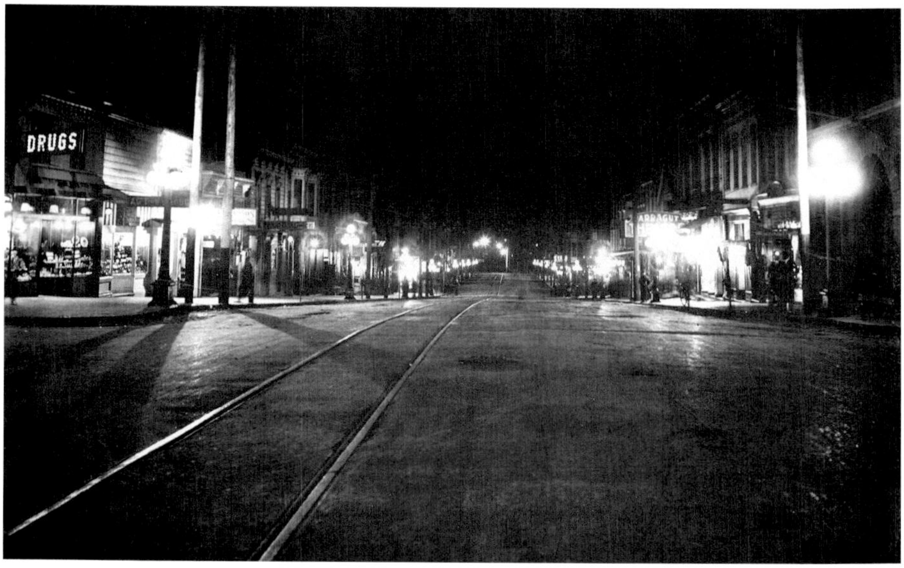

Electric streetlights were installed on Lower Georgia Street in 1913 by the Vallejo Electric Light & Power Co. *[Jack Stiltz collection]*

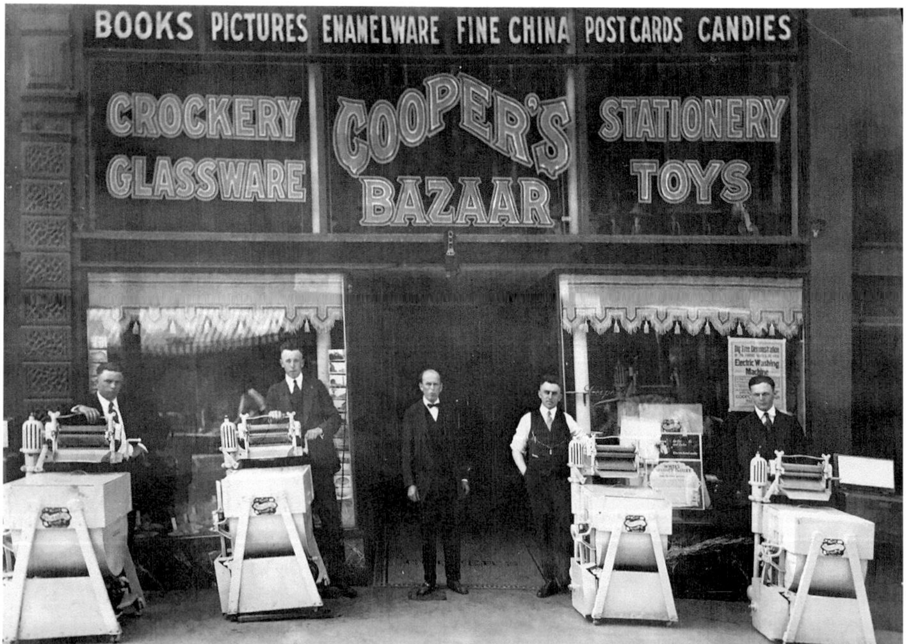

In the early 1900s, Cooper's Bazaar, 229 Georgia St., sold washing machines and other household goods. In World War II, the ground floor was a bar and the upper floor was the Astoria Hotel, described as a brothel by police. *[Vallejo Naval and Historical Museum]*

Even a good football game could be trouble. A March 11, 1909, news story describing how the Oakland Century team wanted to play Vallejo's famed Winged V team—but not in Vallejo because of fears that they would have fight their way out of town. In one game, an *Oakland Tribune* columnist said the Oakland team, on the verge of winning, had to flee when "a flock of cops, volunteer and otherwise, invaded the field" and began hitting the visitors with fists and clubs. The Oakland team had arrived by a chartered steamer, and there was "a wild rush down Georgia Street to the boat and most of the players made the trip in their football regalia, later dressing on the steamer. T'was a rough party of men." The players got steak dinners on their boat ride home, but one, "Ming" Bruzzone, used "a perfectly good raw steak to cover one of his eyes that had been closed by a volunteer cop," the *Tribune* said.

The *Vallejo Evening News* office, on Georgia Street just a block outside the Lower Georgia district, also had its share of excitement. A May 10, 1909, account in the paper described how its publisher, W. D. Pennycook, was struck in the face by Napa lawyer Theodore Bell, angry over harsh editorial criticism directed at him. Bell, a former congressman, got a $5,000 settlement for a client who sued the city in a dispute over a water pipeline right-of-way. Bell also was trying to get a franchise for a ferry to run between Vallejo and Mare Island, and Pennycook editorialized that "a certain Napa lawyer would starve to death were it not for the city of Vallejo." After Bell hit Pennycook, the publisher hit back, knocking off Bell's glasses. "Mr. Bell then had courage to pick up his glasses and the publisher went upstairs," Pennycook wrote in his front-page account. "Here the incident ended."

Times were prosperous, but not for all. The Sept. 21, 1910, *Vallejo Evening Chronicle* reported that Frances Poncini, short on funds because her 101 Georgia St. rooming house wasn't getting much business, decided to set fire to the place and try to collect on a $500 insurance policy. In her confession, printed in the paper, she admitted setting the fire in one room and then going back to her own room "to await the fire alarm to be sounded by someone. My conscience began to bother me so much that after staying in my room about fifteen minutes I rushed back into the burning room and put the fire out which had gained some headway."

By 1914, and the start of World War I in Europe, the number of Vallejo saloons was down to 45, and the *Los Angeles Times,* in a Dec. 12, 1914, story, said the count would be down to 25 by early 1915. The cutback was ordered by the City Council, "instigated by views recently expressed by Secretary of the Navy Josephus Daniels regarding the proximity of so many saloons to Mare Island navy yard," the *Times* account stated. "Seven years ago, 100 saloons existed in Vallejo, until Charles J. Bonaparte, then secretary of the Navy, declared that unless the number materially was reduced he would withhold much government work from Mare Island. Accordingly, the City Council lopped off half the number," the *Times* added.

Among other things, Daniels decided to move a Mare Island receiving ship closer to San Francisco. The *Army and Navy Register* said the "moral tone" of Vallejo figured in Daniel's decision, and the Oct. 18, 1914, *Washington Post* added that the Navy had been dissatisfied with conditions in Vallejo "where many temptations were placed before enlisted men that resulted in breaches of discipline." The Oct. 20, 1914, *Vallejo Evening Chronicle,* responding to the *Register*, said that publication "has long pursued a policy of knocking Mare Island whenever possible and in the present instance its statement and what it implies are as little justified by the facts as in the past." The newspaper said statistics showed that San Francisco had one saloon to 174 residents while Vallejo had one saloon to every 266 residents. "If the desire of the Navy Department is to have a receiving ship maintained at the station where there are the fewest number of saloons it is taking a strange means of accomplishing this by even considering San Francisco," the *Evening Chronicle* said. "The figures in the case speak for themselves."

As for prostitution, the Navy continued to make its demands for an end to vice and local authorities continued to make the usual promises to do so—but Vallejo's brothels were still in business. During mid-1913, the *San Francisco Bulletin* published a serialized account of a prostitute who used the name Alice Smith. The ghostwritten first-person account, described in the 2016 book, *Alice, Memoirs of a Barbary Coast Prostitute*, edited by Ivy Anderson and Devon Angus, generated thousands of letters to the newspaper's editor, Fremont Older. Many of those letters were written by "working girls" from Vallejo who joined in the frank discussion of issues such as abortion, police corruption and the unwritten rules of brothel life.

On June 23, 1913, the same day that Alice Smith's serialized account began running in the *Bulletin*, Vallejo prostitute Lola Garrett testified in Police Court against William Schell, accusing him of leading her into a "sordid and debasing" existence. Her testimony in support of a pimping charge against Schell "was well substantiated by two other scarlet women and three sailors, who gave evidence," the *Vallejo Daily Times* reported the next day. "The story was one of the most dramatic heard in the local courts, and hardened gossip, scandal and sensation mongers, who always make it a point to attend hearings of this description, were moved," the newspaper said. "Not a one that did not pity the handsome slip of a woman gone wrong, and not one that did not believe her story rang true."

The newspaper stories and letters circulated as California lawmakers debated the state's Red Light Abatement Act, a proposal intended to curtail or eliminate prostitution. The Act was passed by the California Legislature in 1913, but a petition drive to cancel the law was launched. Several hundred Vallejoans immediately signed onto the petition, which ultimately failed. The act finally took effect on Nov. 3, 1914, and brothels in many areas of the state were shut down—but not for long in Vallejo.

On April 6, 1917, President Woodrow Wilson asked Congress for a declaration of war against Imperial Germany. Mare Island and Vallejo were about to experience extreme growing pains, and operators of Vallejo's saloons, gambling dens and whorehouses had not heard the last from Secretary of the Navy Daniels, intent on ensuring that nothing interfered with the all-important war effort.

3

World War I and Prohibition

With the 1917 entry of the United States into World War I, Mare Island's workforce grew by leaps and bounds. There were about 3,000 shipyard employees before the nation's declaration of war on Imperial Germany, and the count was up to 5,500 by early 1918. Over the next two years the total soared to about 10,000. Training schools for more than 8,000 sailors and Marines were set up. "Overnight empty houses and spare rooms in Vallejo became a thing of the past," Arnold Lott wrote in *A Long Line of Ships*. "Workmen lived in garages and tents; they commuted from surrounding cities by auto, ferryboat, and interurban trolley. … Saloons, which in Vallejo were outnumbered only by the *filles de joie*, immediately upped the price of beer and began cutting down on the free lunch."

In late August, 1917, a crowd of sailors protested the price increases. "The affair apparently started as a protest against alleged price hikes at the New Crystal Café; but, fed by beer, boredom, and a few bricks, it soon developed into a regular Donnybrook," Lott wrote. Liberty in Vallejo was cut off by the Navy, and the captain of the yard, Commander Joseph Mason Reeves, spelled out the Navy's position: "The elimination of saloons, houses of prostitution, and the illegal sale of liquor to enlisted men, and the establishment of proper and wholesome means of amusement and recreation will be decisive factors in determining whether enlisted men are granted liberty in Vallejo." Reeves was backed by the shipyard commandant, Capt. Harry George, who declared that all saloons in Vallejo had to be closed before sailors could come to town.

The Aug. 28, 1917, *Vallejo Evening Chronicle* said that if the stories of overcharging were true, merchants responsible for the overcharging should have their business licenses revoked immediately. "On the other hand, it is hard that the men should not only lose their liberty to come to this city, but that all business houses should be virtually placed in the same category; that they should be made to suffer for the actions of a few," the newspaper stated.

The Mare Island commandant insisted on the saloon closures. His demand was bannered on the front page of the Sept. 25, 1917, *Vallejo Evening Chronicle,* which quoted him as saying, "If the city does not do it voluntarily it will be forced to do so by the Navy Department, from whom an order to this effect is expected daily. It will not satisfy the department if some of the worst conducted saloons here are put out of business and the others allowed to continue. The clean-up must be absolute." Capt. George also said many sailors were contracting venereal diseases in Vallejo brothels, in addition to getting drunk in the saloons.

George already had seen a report on Vallejo's saloons and whorehouses written by Edwin Grant, a former California state senator who represented the State Law Enforcement and Protective League, a zealous Prohibition advocacy group. A similar report was made by Bascom Johnson, director of the law enforcement division of the new federal Commission on Training Camp Activities. Johnson, who had a key role in closing down prostitution in San Francisco's Barbary Coast, was given the rank of major in the U.S. Army Sanitary Corps. The division's task was to rid areas near military camps and bases of liquor and prostitution problems.

Grant said in his report that he and two other men made an undercover tour of several brothels and saloons in the Lower Georgia district and elsewhere in the Vallejo area on May 19, 1917, a payday for sailors. He reported seeing prostitutes and many young sailors at the locations, and added that he was told the price for a prostitute would be $2. At one house at 231 Santa Clara St., Grant said he sought to avoid suspicion by telling the madam the three men would be back later to stay all night, and she said, "After you get through with the rest of the girls, I'll go you a few rounds."

Johnson included Grant's report in his document, saying copies had gone to newspapers and to various city, county and state officials. "While little or nothing resulted in the way of convictions from this expose, prostitution was made much more difficult to access in Vallejo and the surrounding territory," Johnson added. He also said that E. E. Esdon, secretary of the Naval YMCA, had reported that in a tour of 20 saloons he had "found the bars lined up with mere boys drinking." Esdon also showed Johnson 150 empty beer and whiskey bottles he had picked up around the YMCA building during one month. Johnson said he and another investigator made undercover tours of saloons and suspected brothels in Vallejo, and met women who "offered to commit prostitution with both the investigator and myself." He also reported seeing a few drunken sailors and Marines.

Johnson also said he met with Capt. George and asked that two uniformed sailors be assigned to help him with his investigation, but the commandant "refused this request curtly. He seemed very much annoyed that I had come to him, intimated quite plainly that he did not desire interference of outsiders, as he was perfectly capable of handling the situation himself." Johnson added that Capt. George said that "in his judgment, Vallejo was as clean a town as he had ever seen. … His attitude throughout was hostile and

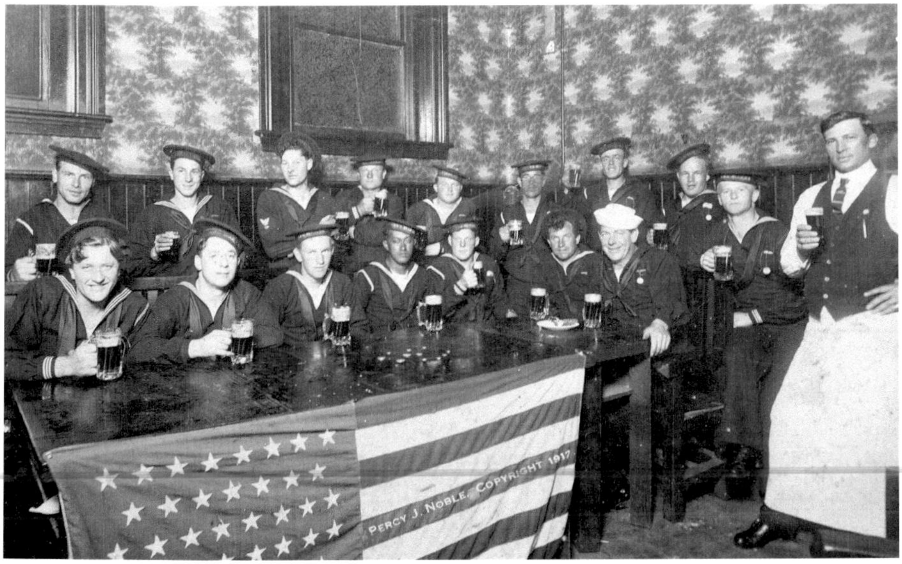

Sailors from the USS *Bear*, at Mare Island Naval Shipyard in 1917, at a Lower Georgia Street bar. The bartender was Jack Stiltz, uncle of Jack Stiltz who served as Vallejo's police chief. *[Jack Stiltz collection]*

contemptuous. I am satisfied from this interview that little can be expected from him in supporting an aggressive campaign to maintain reasonably clean conditions in Vallejo." However, Capt. George later proved himself to be an ally, claiming that Vallejo officials weren't cooperating in the efforts to control vice in the city.

Local business and government leaders tried to work out a solution with the Navy, which included a plan to use Solano County funds to hire detectives who would report directly to the Navy and develop evidence that could lead to successful prosecutions of those involved in "dirty traffic," the *Vallejo Evening Chronicle* reported. But by the end of the month local business owners voted 59-33 against closing the saloons, and Police Chief Stanford followed up in early October with a rejection of Capt. George's claims of non-cooperation. Stanford's Oct. 4, 1917, statement printed in the *Evening Chronicle* included a list of recent police cases, including a man's arrest for selling two bottles of beer to two sailors for 30 cents—exactly what he had paid for the beers. Other, more serious cases dealt with overcharging by merchants, lotteries and prostitution. That proved, he contended, that "all aspersions and reflections upon the zeal of this department in the performance of its duty in this connection or otherwise, and from whatever source, are unjust and absolutely unwarranted by the facts and record."

But the Vallejo business and government leaders were fighting an uphill battle, facing unyielding pressure from the Navy that came straight from Josephus Daniels, President Wilson's teetotaling secretary of the Navy. In *Last Call: The Rise and Fall of Prohibition,* author Daniel Okrent says Daniels' ascension to cabinet rank by Wilson "brought Prohibition sentiment into the highest reaches of the executive branch." While there were high-ranking Navy officers who didn't agree with his sweeping reform efforts, Daniels, dubbed "Sir Josephus, Admiral of the USS *Grapejuice Pinafore*" by the *New York Herald*, was in charge.

Daniels in early 1918 told a local-level ally, Vallejo Councilman J. R. Wilson, that the Navy would be "greatly gratified" if the town's saloons were closed. "I feel and have felt that the most wholesome conditions could not be maintained there until the saloons and other places which lead young men astray are closed," Daniels said, adding he wanted sailors to know "there were no public places in Vallejo which tended to weaken the efficiency of the youth of the Navy."

That polite tone vanished soon afterwards. On March 6, 1918, Secretary Daniels imposed a five-mile zone around all naval bases and stations in the United States in which no liquor could be sold. In his order, Daniels singled out Vallejo, saying the Navy's clean-up efforts "have been stubbornly opposed by those interested in the continuation of this evil and no remedial results of any significance have been realized." Daniels noted he had been advised by Capt. George that he had personally arrested a sailor "in the back room of a disreputable resort known as the Liberty Inn in the heart of Vallejo's business district."

"Vallejo's saloons must close," said the *Vallejo Evening Chronicle* in its front-page report on the edict. "Roadhouses within five miles of Mare Island must also turn to other business. Family liquor stores, restaurants, wholesalers and social clubs in this city must cease all traffic in alcoholic drinks. The five-mile dry zone around Mare Island is an actuality. ... In Vallejo, twenty-two saloons are affected, nine restaurants, four social clubs, two hotels, four wholesale liquor stores, four family liquor stores, while outside the city are seven roadhouses." The *Vallejo Times* added that Daniels' order was hastened by the recommendations from Capt. George, by about 500 Vallejo women who had urged the City Council to take action, and by state and federal investigators.

Critics of the no-booze zone included the Vallejo Chamber of Commerce and the Trades and Labor Council of Vallejo. The Labor Council sent a telegram to Daniels categorizing the charges against Vallejo as "libelous indictments against the patriotic efforts of the people of Vallejo and an assault upon the civil liberties of men who had come here from distant states on account of the war to help build ships."

Editors and publishers of local newspapers had mixed views about the liquor restrictions. The *Vallejo Daily Times'* publisher, Robert W. Walker, came under fire from the *Vallejo Evening News*, run by Henry F. Stahl, for supporting the restrictions in Vallejo while holding an ownership interest in a Napa building that housed a saloon. The *Evening News* accused the *Daily Times* of being the Vallejo "organ of the Prohibitionists" and "working both ends against the middle." In a March 2, 1918, front-page account, the *News* added that it was "strange that the *Times* should fear that the saloons of Vallejo may ruin the enlisted men, but never has a word to say of the sailors and marines going to Napa and not only drinking but getting drunk. Vallejoites visiting Napa have witnessed more drunken sailors and marines on the streets of that town in one night than were ever observed here in a month. And for all we know, the little saloon in the Walker property may be responsible for some of it."

The *Evening News* also backed the protest sent to Navy Secretary Daniels by the Trades and Labor Council of Vallejo, but Daniels was unmovable. He set March 16 as the deadline for the last drink. As the deadline neared, the Samoset Glee Club paraded a coffin filled with beer bottles through the town. It was payday on Mare Island, and yard employees swarmed into the Vallejo saloons to drink. "Up to the final fleeting minute, the saloons were packed to their sidewalls, so that, when the exodus came, there were more people on the street than have been there in the memory of the oldest inhabitant," the *San Francisco Examiner* reported. "Many of those who held their feet on the old familiar rail until the last availed themselves of the opportunity to buy drinks at bargain rates, the saloons all conducting auctions of their stock, and selling, in some instances, at as low as ten per cent of the ruling market price. They brought suitcases with them and chartered jitneys for the emergency delivery service. Others came out to the sidewalk, bottles in hand and drank the contents there and then broke the bottles in the street." The next day there was no liquor available within five miles of the Navy yard, but traffic on roads leading to nearby Benicia and Napa, outside the zone, "showed a definite increase," *Long Line of Ships* author Arnold Lott wrote.

Edwin Grant of the State Law Enforcement and Protective League was in full support of Daniels' efforts. Grant, following up on his 1917 undercover tour and damning report, claimed he saw sailors in Vallejo "reeling drunk upon the public streets in sight of the police, who did nothing," a Feb. 25, 1918, *Santa Cruz Evening Chronicle* article stated. "He obtained evidence against one of these places (the Liberty Inn) in which a prominent brewer of Vallejo and member of a state commission owns an interest, and brought charges against it before the council, which declined to act upon them."

The brewer targeted by Grant was prominent Vallejoan Henry J. Widenmann, a state highway commissioner, former state assemblyman and Solano County supervisor, and potential U.S. House candidate who with his brother, Adolph, owned the Solano Brewery. Other than Grant's claim, there's no indication that Henry Widenmann held an interest in the Liberty Inn. The Vallejo-born brothers had taken over the brewery from their father, Charles, a German immigrant who started the business in 1854, the same year Farragut established Mare Island Naval Shipyard. Henry Widenmann had worked with local authorities on ways to clean up tavern operations. He wanted to sue Grant, a state senator when Widenmann was in the Assembly, for slander but his lawyer advised against it. On March 9, 1918, he and his brother spotted Grant and the Rev. H. G. Porter of Vallejo leaving a newspaper office near the brewery and getting into a car. The *Vallejo Evening Chronicle* reported that Henry Widenmann walked over to the car, accused Grant of making personal accusations against him, and called him a liar and "miserable cúr." All four men "went to clinches," the *San Francisco Chronicle* reported in its version of the incident. Grant's organization along with the Vallejo Dry Association and the Women's Christian Temperance Union were highly critical of the Widenmanns and of Mayor James Roney, saying he was present when the incident occurred but "stood idly by." Roney rejected the claim that he was at the scene, calling it "an unqualified, malicious and inexcusable falsehood."

Following the confrontation, Henry Widenmann said he was so offended by Grant's repeated inferences that he was a traitorous "agent of the Kaiser's" that he was compelled to "chastise Mr. Grant physically. … I am American through and through. I am most heartily in sympathy with the cause of the country of my birth, and I dare any man to question my loyalty to my country."

"As to the liquor business, I am done," Widenmann said, adding that he was dismantling the Solano Brewery and starting another business even though it would be hard on the family's finances. That new business was the Solano Ice Cream Company, which opened around the corner from the old brewery.

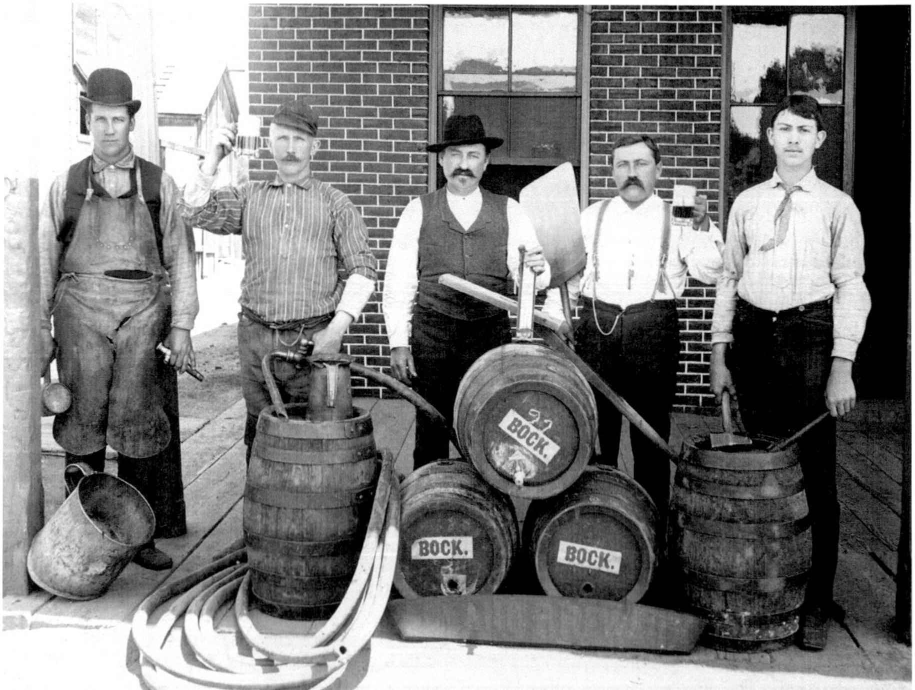

Solano Brewery owners Henry Widenmann, second from right, his brother, Adolph, center, and three employees in front of the brewery in downtown Vallejo in the early 1900s. *[Vallejo Naval and Historical Museum]*

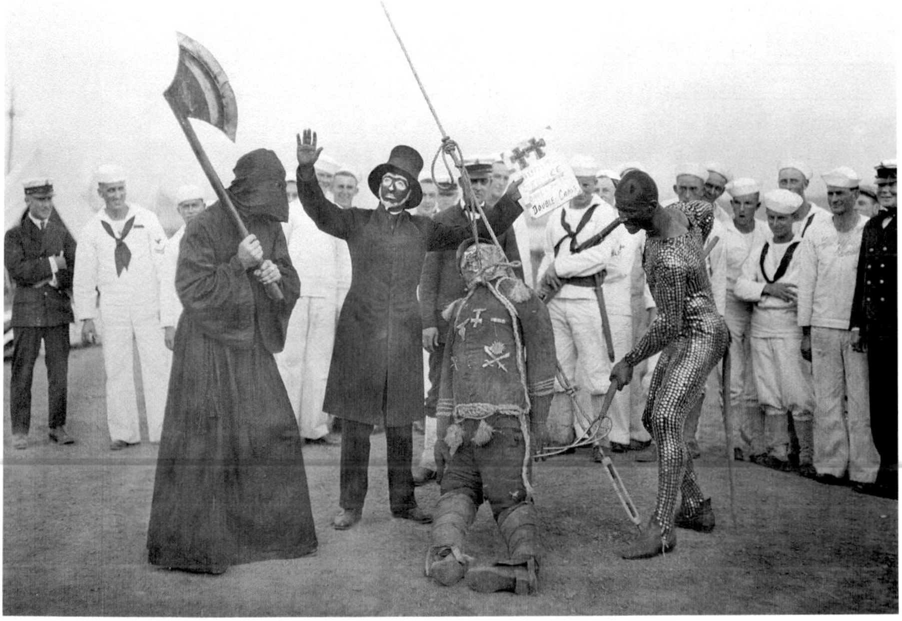

In this photo, taken on Mare Island in 1918, characters representing the Grim Reaper, an undertaker and the Devil hang German's Kaiser Wilhelm in effigy. Anti-German sentiment ran high in the United States during World War I. *[Vallejo Naval and Historical Museum]*

If Widenmann was targeted by Grant and other "dry" advocates, he had strong support from other Vallejo business owners and from some newspapers, including the *Sacramento Bee,* which editorialized that the "drys" were in the wrong and were known to "twist and warp the slightest circumstances in order to add fuel to the flames of their cause." The *Mountain Messenger,* in Downieville, California, took it a step further, saying that if Grant "only got a bruised nose and a blackened optic he has no kick coming and is lucky to get off as easily as he did. The truth is Grant is a fanatic of the worst kind, and the only thing that will bring these animals to their senses is severe physical punishment administered by an expert."

When Widenmann appeared in court on a battery charge stemming from the incident, the penalty was a light slap on the wrist: Justice J. A. Fitzgerald imposed a sentence of 24 hours of probation, and praised Widenmann for being "a peaceful and law-abiding citizen" with "known loyalty to the United States" and "sterling qualities as a gentleman."

Grant's criticism of the Widenmanns paralleled a national strategy of xenophobic fear-mongering by proponents of Prohibition. In *Last Call,* Okrent said Prohibition advocates needed 36 states for ratification of their constitutional amendment, and to ensure ratification they took full advantage of "a rising tide of strong anti-German feelings sweeping across the country." That included views of German-American brewers as "tools of the Kaiser." That rising tide drew strength from President Wilson, whose "own war-making propaganda was built around anti-European, particularly anti-German, feeling," Okrent writes. He added that the president, in preparing the nation for the war he wanted it to enter, "set out to demonize some of those Americans who were 'born under other flags' but who had 'poured the poison of disloyalty into the very arteries of our national life.'"

Capt. George, mirroring Edwin Grant in appealing to the anti-German feeling, criticized both Widenmann and another well-known Vallejoan, Adolph W. Stremmel, who ran the Liberty Inn at 412 Georgia St. "This Liberty Inn, formerly the Heidelberg Inn, has changed its name, but not its business," George said. "It is kept by a German who is a henchman of a brewer, a German, who is reputed to practically control the saloon element of Vallejo and the municipal government, and I have had these premises under suspicion for a long time and have reported my observations to the Bureau of Investigation, Department of Justice, San Francisco."

Capt. George also was strongly opposed to the various forms of gambling that Navy sailors encountered while on liberty in Vallejo. That resulted in a war of words between him and Vallejo Police Judge John Browne, known as "Judge Ha Ha" because of his humorous asides, both in private and public. In a Nov. 1, 1918, court decision, Browne imposed a small $10 fine on Fong Chow for running a Chinese lottery in the Lower Georgia Street district, according to an account in the December 1990 *Solano Historian*. Browne also accused Navy investigators who developed the case of trying to "purify" Vallejo while shipyard officials were running their own gambling games in the form of raffles to promote sales of "Liberty Loan" bonds. At the same time, Browne ruled in two other Navy-initiated cases to suspend judgment in one and continue the other.

An irate Capt. George followed up with a lengthy letter on Nov. 26, 1918, that Navy investigators had turned up enough evidence to justify arrests of 25 people, most in the Lower Georgia district, for violations of various laws. But George said Browne's courtroom actions revealed that the Navy "cannot look for assistance to the judicial authorities of Vallejo in compelling obedience to the law." He added:

> The Commandant is not trying to purify Vallejo, and the morals of the residents of that community are largely a matter of indifference. He does, however, propose to thoroughly protect the enlisted men attached to this Station from gamblers, crooks, blacklegs and other disreputable parasites of society who flock to the neighborhood of camps. The Commandant is surprised that you, as presiding Judge of a court of law, should have seen fit to place the officials of this Navy yard, who were not on trial, on a parity with gamblers and blacklegs. The inability to draw a distinction between petty gambling and the methods pursued at this Navy Yard to arouse enthusiasm for and give publicity to national enterprises for patriotic purposes indicates a temperamental unfitness to perform judicial duties.

In a lengthy Dec. 31, 1918, response filled with overblown, rambling rhetoric, Browne said he checked with the federal Treasury Department regarding Mare Island shipyard raffles to promote Liberty Bond sales and was advised that the agency didn't countenance such activity since "lotteries of any nature are contrary to law." The judge said that the "Purity Squad" on Mare Island wasn't doing anything about the shipyard workers playing "the seductive game of 'Craps,' the stakes running from a collar button to a Liberty Bond." He also told Capt. George that as "an abettor of gambling you appear raw and astringent as the ordinary 'craps shooter' creating the conditions calling for the comment. Though eminent in command the court nevertheless is impelled to admonish you."

It didn't end there. Browne said he wanted to avoid "any personal reflection"—and then told Capt. George that "several decades ago as an Ensign on the *Independence* to the street world of the old town you were known as the 'Rough-neck Ensign from the Guardo'—through the nightly or frequent orgies of disreputable associations and reprehensible actions ... you were a strange compound of officer probity and public grossness." Browne concluded by saying, "For the New Year may your syntactical ballistics never fall short in hitting the right head, in its measure for purity."

World War I ended on Nov. 11, 1918, and within a few months 1,500 Mare Island sailors were discharged and about 5,500 shipyard employees found themselves out of a job. But Lott wrote in *Long Line of Ships* that the local economy held up better than might have been expected because the Pacific Fleet, even with cutbacks, was bigger than it had been before the war. There was enough ship repair and overhaul work to keep Mare Island going. That was good news for Vallejo as well, although the saloon-keepers' difficulties didn't end. Now they faced a new problem: Prohibition.

Prohibition in a Shipyard Town

In December 1917, the 18th Amendment, prohibiting the "manufacture, sale, or transportation of intoxicating liquors for beverage purposes," was passed by Congress and sent to the states for ratification. In January 1919, the 18th amendment achieved the necessary two-thirds majority of state ratification, and prohibition became the law of the land. The Volstead Act, passed nine months later, provided for the enforcement of prohibition, and in January 1920 Vallejo's saloons joined their counterparts across the country in no longer selling liquor. At least, that's what they said for the record.

Prohibition had been a long time coming. In *Last Call*, Okrent traces the roots of Prohibition to what's known as the Washingtonian Movement, which arose out of a Baltimore barroom in 1840 and mushroomed into the nation's first large-scale expression of anti-alcohol sentiment. The "dry" movement grew slowly even as the number of saloons in America continued to increase, from about 100,000 in 1870 to nearly 300,000 in 1900.

The "drys" included people like Carrie Nation, who, Okrent says, "was six feet tall, with the biceps of a stevedore, the face of a prison warden, and the persistence of a toothache." Visiting Cincinnati at the peak of her renown, Nation was asked why she hadn't wielded her signature hatchet to smash booze bottles in the city's saloons. Her reply, Okrent says, "would have been just as apt in dozens of American cities." Vallejo, with its 100 or so saloons in the Lower Georgia district in the early 1900s, certainly qualified for the list. Nation's comment: "I would have dropped from exhaustion before I had gone a block."

Carrie Nation and other proponents of Prohibition were wedded to proponents of the universal suffrage amendment, in what Okrent describes as "an expedient relativism" rather than "any moral congruence." He added that exponents of that connection included "one of America's least likely advocates of Prohibition, the novelist Jack London." The hard-drinking writer remains the most famous member of the Vallejo Yacht Club, which he joined in 1910 and where he kept his 30-foot sailboat, *Roamer*. London, in his *John Barleycorn: Alcoholic Memoirs*, said he voted for a California woman suffrage proposition in 1911, convinced that "the moment women get the vote in any community, the first thing they proceed to do is close the saloons." London, who had several drinks before and after that vote, added that he would finally be able to stop drinking "when no one else drinks and when no drink is obtainable." London wanted the suffragists to vote him into sobriety, Okrent said, adding that the author's insight into the dry campaign's dependence on the suffrage movement was "incontrovertible."

> Not only had the suffrage movement found its most effective generals among women who had first developed their political skills in the temperance ranks; additionally, thousands of women in the WCTU had come to realize that no anti-alcohol weapon could be as potent as the franchise. What had changed by the time London cast his wishfully opportunistic suffrage vote was the nature of the connection between the drys and the suffragists: comfortable affinity had been transformed into absolute interdependence.

Enforcement of the Prohibition amendment resulted in many arrests and penalties for bootlegging and other liquor-related crimes in Vallejo, most of them in the Lower Georgia Street zone. Accounts of those crimes ran in newspapers throughout the years that Prohibition remained in force, before finally ending on Dec. 5, 1933. Arthur Lindauer, Solano County district attorney from 1914 to 1922, promised to prosecute every case reported to him. But enforcement of Prohibition was difficult given an ingrained Navy "liberty town" culture that thrived in Vallejo. The enforcers' task wasn't made any easier by comments by some public officials and by news accounts that played on a view held by many that Prohibition was a bad idea, maybe even a joke.

The mocking critics included Vallejo Police Judge John Browne, Jack London's good friend and the same "Judge Ha Ha" who had suggested the Navy was being hypocritical

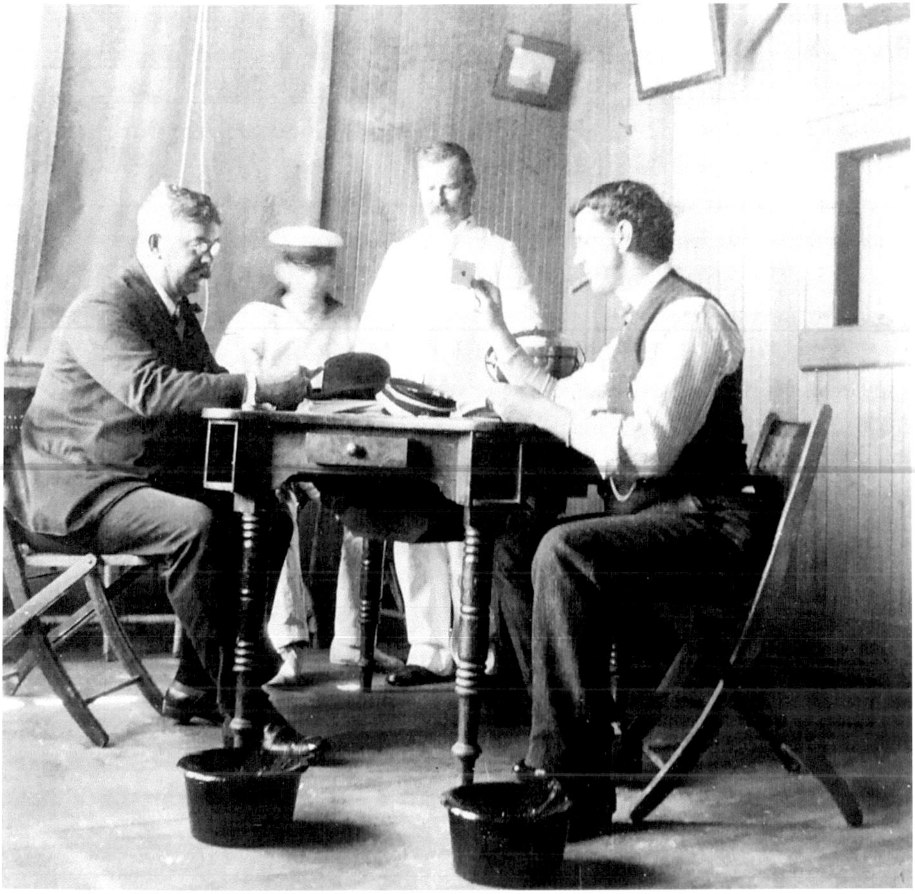

Author Jack London plays cards with George Hilton at the Vallejo Yacht Club. London's friend, Judge Browne, standing in center, keeps an eye on the game. *[Vallejo Naval and Historical Museum]*

in its anti-gambling stance. In a front-page Oct. 31, 1921, article, the *Vallejo Evening Chronicle* said Browne had proposed a contract between the city and the Vallejo Yacht Club that would enable the club to buy contraband booze seized in police raids. The liquor could be used to remove barnacles and old paint from boats, said Browne, an active yacht club member. "After endangering his olfactory organs this morning while determining that certain evidence in bottles was indeed 'likker,' Judge Browne declared that the stuff would quickly remove barnacles and paint from copper bottoms of boats but would have to be removed quickly if the owners of the boats want to save the hulls," the article stated.

Judge Browne's proposed contract was just a joke, but the Yacht Club still had a way to get liquor without anyone noticing. Club member and longtime Vallejoan Tom Ochs says his father, Ralph Ochs, also a Yacht Club member, and Joe Schlosser, for many years the

three arrests in the Lower Georgia Street district and two in Benicia; and a March 17, 1930, raid by federal prohibition at five Vallejo locations, three of them in the Lower Georgia Street district, resulting in the arrests of seven people on bootlegging charges. Another raid reported on Nov. 24, 1931, resulted in one arrest on liquor possession charges at another Lower Georgia location; and a Nov. 16, 1932, news story reported the arrests of five alleged bootleggers at separate Lower Georgia Street locations.

While most of the news accounts were brief, others ran longer and contained some interesting details. A federal raid reported in the *Vallejo Evening Chronicle* on June 11, 1932, resulted in the arrests of seven men, all with businesses in the 100 and 200 blocks of Georgia Street, on liquor offenses. Each was fined $100. Members of a citizens' group then urged city council members to cancel the business licenses held by the men, but that meeting grew testy when one delegation member, Guy Hale, said, "If you gentlemen can't handle these matters, we will have to go to other sources." Mayor Fred Heegler didn't like what he heard, telling Hale, "It ill becomes you to appear here and make a veiled threat of that kind." Hale quickly apologized.

An April 3, 1921, story, mentioned in Arnold Lott's *Long Line of Ships*, dealt with an investigation into the theft of 200 gallons of alcohol from the paint shop on Mare Island. A Navy lieutenant faced a court martial on a charge of conspiring to steal the alcohol and sell it to bootleggers in San Francisco, but in the end was cleared. The officer became a suspect because he had acquired some large cans that could have been used to transport the alcohol, but explained that he was going to haul gasoline in the cans on a planned road trip.

The *Vallejo Evening Chronicle* had a Feb. 5, 1929, story about a cabbie employed at a Lower Georgia Street taxi stand being arrested by shipyard authorities for not only providing liquor to a Marine, but also delivering the booze to the Marine barracks on Mare Island. The Marine who asked for the delivery was also arrested.

Other sources of liquor included small stills "all over town," according to Vallejo native Ray Bowman, who said those stills included one that his father, Al Bowman, had in his backyard in the early 1930s. "The guys who had them were small-time, they just did it to make a few bucks on the side," Ray Bowman said. "I don't think they had anything to do with selling to the bars in town. They would just make a little batch and sell it to their regular customers." Bowman added that his father would take him along for a night-time ride in the family's Essex car "to see a friend. He would see that friend—and then he would make a stop at another friend's house. Later, I realized he was delivering alky, in five-gallon cans. I remember my mother helping him unload the alky. She was only five feet tall, and the cans she was carrying would almost be touching the ground." Al Bowman's stint as a small-time bootlegger followed what his son described as heavy gambling in a Georgia Street basement cardroom during the 1920s that wiped out an inheritance of about $50,000 that he received. In 1943, ten years after the repeal of Prohibition, Al Bowman was appointed a city constable and held that position until his death in 1951.

Jodean Spinelli Coakley relates one of the more amusing Prohibition-era stories about her grandmother, Frances Castagnoli: For years she would tell how her husband Louis had a still in the early 1930s and learned that "dry" agents were about to conduct a raid. He briefly dropped out of sight, leaving her to deal with the agents. Frances wound up going to court on a bootlegging charge, "and when she went before the judge, guess what? The judge recognized her and said, 'Oh, hi, Mrs. Castagnoli,' and dismissed the case. He was one of her husband's customers," Coakley said. "She would tell that story every Christmas around the dinner table."

Ed Burgle says his father, longtime Vallejo car dealer and duck hunter Gene Burgle, would put on "duck feeds" for his customers and friends and during Prohibition found an innovative way to get lots of the birds without shooting them. "My father had a good friend, Rawson Knight, whose family had a ranch just north of Vallejo, along the Napa River. They had a whiskey still on an island, and they would toss the leftover mash from the still in the water. The ducks would be eating all that grain, and they would pretty much be swimming in circles after a while," Burgle said. "He would row out and fill gunny sacks with drunk ducks, and then would put on these duck feeds." Burgle also said that if the still on Knight Island, a marshy area along the Napa River and Dutchman Slough, was about to be raided, the Knights would get a warning call from the sheriff's office and would have enough time to dismantle the still. His story was confirmed by Lew Carlton, nephew of Rawson Knight.

Besides the liquor-related stories, there were continuing reports of criminal activity in the Lower Georgia Street district that included a murder, rioting that left one dead, an opium bust and prostitution-related arrests. A Nov. 4, 1927, report in the *Petaluma Argus-Courier* described the murder of Frank Smernes in his Athens poolroom at 137 Georgia St. A business partner, James Lazarus, was charged with shooting Smernes four times after Smernes struck him during an argument over a card game. Lazarus fled but was captured in South Vallejo. While he was being booked at the city jail, Tony Smernes, cousin of the dead man, showed up at the station with a revolver and threatened to shoot Lazarus, but was disarmed by officers. Lazarus, who said he didn't remember anything after Smernes hit him, was well known to local authorities. A Sept. 24, 1923, story in the *Vallejo Evening Chronicle* described his arrest at his 105 Georgia St. soft drink business on gambling charges.

A March 5, 1921, *Vallejo Evening Chronicle* report described how a late-night fight in the Lower Georgia district between two Marines and five sailors turned into a riot when more men joined in—so many that "members from the provost guard from the navy yard were powerless to stop the trouble. Police and provost guards were helpless and not until both sides had been fought out did the rumpus end." The brawl left five men in need of medical help. One, a Marine private, suffered a fractured skull and died three days later.

The *Vallejo Evening Chronicle* ran a Sept. 20, 1923, story about three Chinese men being arrested at a Marin Street location, just outside the Lower Georgia district, by officers who found "a large quantity of opium, other drugs and smoking equipment." One of the men had run a laundry in Vallejo for many years while another was a naval steward stationed on Mare Island.

Authorities continued to deal with prostitution-related cases. An April 11, 1924, story in the *Oakland Tribune* told how a woman was given a sentence of 250 days in jail or a $250 fine for running a "disorderly house." The judge said the sentence would be suspended "if the woman agreed to leave town in eight hours." A Sept. 25, 1923, report in the *Vallejo Evening Chronicle* said another woman in the Lower Georgia district was charged with vagrancy and fined $20. She was arrested at 134B Virginia St., described by police as a "known disorderly house as well as a bootlegging establishment."

The Great Experiment Comes to an End

The day before the Dec. 5, 1933, end of the Prohibition era, the *Vallejo Times-Herald* editorialized about the need for responsibility by businesses that would soon have the legal right to serve liquor. "The chief trouble with the old-time saloon wasn't the fact that men stood up to drink, or that their drinks were shoved at them across a polished bit of mahogany," the *Times-Herald* said. "It was that the saloon—as an institution—had precious little discretion. It sold, in most cases, to anyone who could lay a coin on the bar—to chronic drunkards, to spendthrifts, to flighty youngsters, and to men whose families were in want."

"There were saloonkeepers, of course, who had some sense of responsibility in these matters, but they were the exceptions. In the main, the corner saloon was nearly all that the prohibitionists said it was. A liquor control law which permits any kind of public drinking must be framed with that in mind. Details of the sale—whether it be at a table or over a bar—are unimportant. It is the spirit in which the traffic as a whole is handled that counts."

Another editorial ran in the newspaper the next day, as repeal of the Great Experiment took effect, saying, "The people of the nation have been given back the responsibility of dealing with this problem in a temperate manner. Local laws and regulations will have to be worked out in such a manner that the people, by their conduct in the future, will justify their action of repealing the Eighteenth Amendment. We believe they are capable of doing that."

During Prohibition the "unspeakable saloon" disappeared, the *Times-Herald* said. "But in its stead there sprung up no less than 200,000 speakeasies in the nation and, in a very short time, these formed the framework and the background for gangsterism and racketeering that have no equal in history. The American people very clearly indicated, during this period, that they still desired certain beverages and would have them."

A front-page story in the Dec. 6, 1933, *Times-Herald* detailed the Prohibition repeal process, which ended with Utah becoming the 36th state to support repeal. That was the minimum needed to end an era that lasted 13 years, 10 months, and 19 days—an era that was "dry" in name only. Also on the front page was President Roosevelt's plea for temperance and for elimination of bootlegging. "I trust in the good sense of the American people that they will not bring upon themselves the curse of excessive use of intoxicating liquors, to the detriment of health, morals and social integrity," Roosevelt said, adding that Americans should cooperate in seeing that the nation didn't return to "the repugnant conditions that obtained prior to adoption of the 18th Amendment and those that have existed since its adoption."

The Dec. 7, 1933, *Times-Herald's* front-page "It's Ritch" column, written by city editor Jim Ritch, had a good follow-up: "What becomes of racketeering after our liberation from prohibition's rubber handcuffs is the question which bothers John Citizen right now, much more than how unrestrained will the public be since the restrictions are removed by repeal." The hope is that the "brass knuckle and machine gun lords" will be gone, Ritch said, adding, "Everybody hopes it will, for the average citizen was probably more fed up with a system where desperadoes could become fabulously rich from crime and still enjoy the tolerance of the public and the law, as he was fed up with the legal repressions of prohibition."

Okrent, in *Last Call*, says Prohibition succeeded in one critical respect: as a direct result of its 14-year reign, "Americans drank less. In fact, they continued to drink less for decades afterward." But other than that, he concluded:

> In almost every respect imaginable, Prohibition was a failure. It encouraged criminality and institutionalized hypocrisy. It deprived the government of revenue, stripped the gears of the political system, and imposed profound limitations on individual rights. It fostered a culture of bribery, blackmail, and official corruption. It also maimed and murdered, its excesses apparent in deaths by poison, by the brutality of ill-trained, improperly supervised enforcement officers, and by unfortunate proximity to mob gun battles. One could rightfully replace our prevailing images of Prohibition—flappers kicking up their heels in nightclubs, say, or lawmen swinging axes at barrels of impounded beer—with different visions: maybe the bloated bodies of the hijacked rumrunners washing up on the beach at Martha's Vineyard, their eyes gouged out and their hands and faces scoured by acid. Or perhaps the crippled men of Wichita, their lives devastated by the nerve-destroying chemicals suspended in a thirty-five-cent bottle of Jake.

4

"Big Tobe" Williams, Vallejo's Gangland Connection

The many accounts of bootlegging and other criminal activity on Lower Georgia demonstrate clearly what the district was like during the Prohibition era. But that activity was overshadowed in 1935, two years after Prohibition ended, by the disclosure that George "Baby Face" Nelson and other infamous gangsters had been hanging out in Vallejo. During part of the time that he was in and out of Vallejo, Nelson was the FBI's Public Enemy No. 1. The gangsters' connection was Thomas "Tobe" Williams, a one-legged ex-con who ran the town's only hospital, Vallejo General Hospital, on Tennessee Street, about a dozen city blocks from the Lower Georgia district. The hospital's reputation as a stopping place for notorious criminals wasn't widely known until the details emerged in federal court proceedings in San Francisco. Williams was one of several people rounded up in Northern California and Nevada and charged with harboring Nelson while he was on the run. The harboring trial was big news in papers around the country and put Vallejo in a bad light—a city that had made important national contributions as the home of Mare Island Naval Shipyard but was plagued by a persistent criminal presence.

"Tobe" Williams, born in 1862 in Boston and raised in San Francisco, was an enigma. He was in Vallejo by 1887, but in mid-1900 got a three-year term in the Montana State Prison for burglary. He was released six months early, on Dec. 23, 1902. His right leg had been amputated above the knee, and one story was that he lost the leg and two fingers from his right hand in a bungled attempt to blast open a safe in a Montana bank—a crime that led to his prison time in that state. Little is known about his activities between the time he was released and his 1914 purchase of Vallejo's first hospital, which had been founded seven years earlier by Dr. James Hogan at the corner of Virginia Street and Sonoma Boulevard. In 1922, with community support and a local bank loan, Williams opened a new, larger hospital on Tennessee Street that served the community for decades. But Williams was much more than a hospital owner and manager. Besides serving residents of

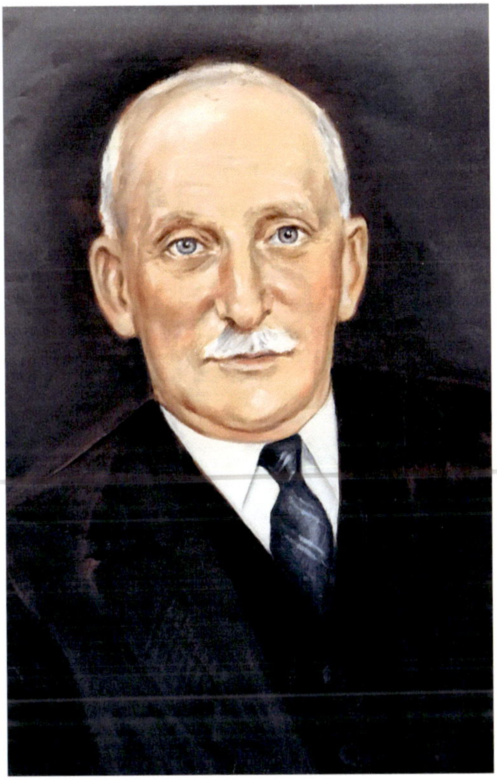

A painting done for "Big Tobe" Williams fits with the image that Williams sought to convey in Vallejo: A respected hospital administrator rather than the ex-convict who was convicted of harboring "Baby Face" Nelson. *[Vallejo Naval and Historical Museum]*

Vallejo, his hospital took care of sick or wounded fugitives who didn't have to worry about being bothered by local authorities. Williams, according to FBI reports, said he had good political connections in Vallejo and would be quickly alerted if any federal authorities were coming to town. In *Baby Face Nelson, Portrait of a Public Enemy*, authors Steven Nickel and William J. Helmer wrote that Williams had become "the unofficial financier for much of the West Coast's bootlegging business." To his underworld pals, the 6'7" Williams was known as "Big Tobe." Gangsters and bootleggers meeting with Williams for the first time were advised in advance to tell him they wanted to see "the gonif from Galway." Those code words translate roughly to "Irish thief," although Williams was Jewish. His birth name was Tobias C. Cohen.

Some Vallejo residents knew or had heard rumors about Williams' background and associations. Pearl Jones Tranter, from a prominent local family, described how her mother explained why Pearl was born in an Oakland hospital rather than Vallejo General: her mother wanted nothing to do with a hospital run by such a shady character. Dr. Edward A. Peterson, in an FBI interview, recalled a conversation with hospital nurse Lorena Slater, who said, "It is the most terrible thing I have ever heard that the boss should allow people like that ('Baby Face' Nelson) to come in here." Peterson also said the nurse referred to Alvin "Creepy" Karpis, a Barker-Karpis gang leader who had his tonsils removed at Vallejo General in February 1933, as one of the "bums" that Williams allowed into the hospital. Dr. Peterson also told the FBI in his Jan. 16, 1935, interview that he and Williams talked about Nelson's status as Public Enemy No. 1, and Williams told him, "The government will never take him alive."

Lorena Slater told the FBI that when she went to work at the hospital she knew that Williams' reputation "was not good, and since then I have seen many things in the way of transactions about the hospital which would indicate that his reputation is questionable." Among other things, the nurse said that during Prohibition the accounts of patients at the hospital "were charged out, as far as the books were concerned, with liquor (legal for medicinal purposes) which they did not receive. This liquor was undoubtedly sold to other people." The nurse also said she witnessed deliveries by bootleggers of what she "surmised to be whiskey" going into Williams' office. While there were plenty of liquor deliveries in the Lower Georgia district during Prohibition, Williams was never charged with any bootlegging activity.

According to a 1935 FBI report, Nelson, who used the aliases "Jimmy Burnell," "James Rogers" and "Jimmy Williams," regularly stopped to visit Williams while traveling between California and Nevada, trying to evade authorities or transporting liquor to Reno. Nelson was hauling booze for Joe Parente, alleged king of the Pacific Coast rum-running industry during Prohibition. Besides Karpis, the FBI's fourth and last Public Enemy No. 1 after Nelson's death, Nelson's wife Helen was a patient at the hospital twice. Her first hospital stay was in 1932 for a D&C procedure, typically associated with miscarriages, and the second time was in 1934 for an examination of her abdominal organs. A federal agent walked into the hospital on Oct. 11, 1934, and saw Barker gang member Chuck Fitzgerald, who was recovering from a gunshot wound, but failed to recognize him at the time. In late 1933, Arthur "Doc" Barker was treated for a wound that caused one of his fingers to get infected. Other patients included Reno underworld figures Bill "Curly" Graham, treated for syphilis, Jim "Shorty" McKay, treated for "relapsing fever," and Henry "Tex" Hall, treated for ulcers. Dr. Peterson told the FBI that in talking with Williams about some of the patients, "I questioned him closely regarding the identity of certain of these persons" and Williams "merely told me that they were racketeers from Chicago. In all these cases the bills were paid in cash, and were usually paid by 'Tobe' Williams himself to me." Kate "Ma" Barker also visited Williams in Vallejo, according to the FBI. She and her son Fred were killed in a Jan. 15, 1935, shootout with fifteen FBI agents in Ocklawaha, FL. Others who stopped from time to time to see Williams included bootlegger Joe "Soap" Moreno and Joseph "Fatso" Negri, who had been a trusted member of Nelson's gang.

Williams and three co-defendants were convicted April 5, 1935, of harboring Nelson. After denouncing organized crime and tolerance of it by some individuals, Federal Judge

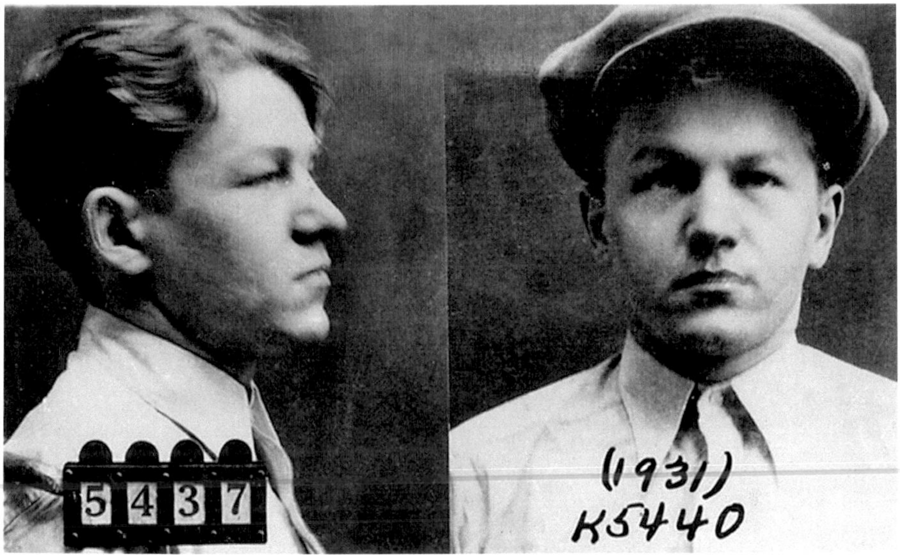

This mugshot of "Baby Face" Nelson was taken in 1931 when he was sentenced to prison in Illinois for robbery. Nelson, the FBI's "Public Enemy No. 1," made many stops in Vallejo. *[Illinois State Bureau of Criminal Identification and Investigation]*

Walter Lindley imposed the harshest sentence on Williams: a $5,000 fine and an 18-month prison term. He was sentenced to prison despite offering a petition signed by 119 Vallejo residents, many of them city officials, asking for clemency on the ground that he was not guilty of harboring "of his own free will and accord." The petition described him as "a man of sterling character, charitable to the needy, and fair to his fellow man." Williams was released after serving a year in McNeil Island federal prison in Washington state.

"Soap" Moreno, one of Williams' co-defendants, got a six-month jail sentence. "Fatso" Negri, a government witness in the harboring trial, was placed on five years' probation. Moreno also was indicted, along with Joe Parente, on separate charges of conspiring to smuggle liquor. That indictment stemmed from a 1932 machine gun battle with authorities at Salt Point in Sonoma County during an attempt to land a boatload of booze offloaded from a Canadian syndicate's smuggling ship. Authorities believed Nelson was the smugglers' triggerman.

Federal investigators, who had wiretaps in the hospital, were interested in more than a list of patients and visitors who were gangsters or associates of the criminals. They also sought unsuccessfully to link the Nelson gang to the Nov. 12, 1934, death of hospital nurse Myrtle Jordan, found lying on a Vallejo street, the victim of an apparent hit-and-run accident. She had been hit several blocks from the home of a patient she had visited. The investigators suspected that the nurse may have been killed because she knew too much about the gangsters' activities. Investigators also looked into the possibility that Roy Frisch, a Reno bank cashier who disappeared on March 22, 1934, just before he was to testify in New York in the mail fraud case of Graham and McKay, was killed near Vallejo. His body was never found. Author Bryan Burroughs wrote in his 2004 book *Public Enemies* that FBI informants said "Nelson murdered Fritsch and dumped his corpse down a mineshaft."

Testimony presented to the U.S. Senate's Special Committee to Investigate Organized Crime in Interstate Commerce, chaired by Sen. Estes Kefauver, described Bill Graham and Jim McKay as "two of the most influential men in the Reno gambling set-up" who after three federal court trials in New York City were convicted in 1938 of using the mails to defraud in a $2.5 million horse race swindle. They were sentenced to nine years in federal prison and fined $11,000 each. A report to Kefauver's committee stated that Graham and McKay "dangled huge but fictitious race track winnings before their victims and told them the cash was theirs if they put up the necessary "good faith" money. In each case the money was placed and "lost" on the wrong horse on the first bet. The victims were rushed out of Reno after the swindle.

When Nelson's wife was hospitalized, he stayed in the Casa de Vallejo, the town's best hotel a few blocks from the Lower Georgia district. Negri told FBI agents that he and the Nelsons also stayed at the Dodgin Auto Court in Vallejo, several blocks from the hospital, in late September and early October, 1934, and while there they walked downtown to see a movie before driving to Reno. On their way to Reno, the Nelsons and Negri realized they accidentally took a blanket from the auto court and stopped to call the auto court owners to tell them they were returning it from Sacramento via parcel post.

Nelson, using the alias "James Rogers," also paid $900 for a new 1934 Plymouth while in Vallejo. According to the FBI, Nelson bought the car from a local Plymouth dealer, Ray Hitchcock, on Jan. 16, 1934, with $100 in cash and an $800 cashier's check. Nelson traded it in a week later in San Francisco for a new Hudson "8." He had to kick in another $336 to close the Hudson deal. Ed Burgle says his father, Gene Burgle, an auto dealer for years, told how Nelson walked into his Vallejo business, one block from Hitchcock's location, and said he wanted a car and had the money to buy it. The two began haggling over prices and Burgle, unaware of his customer's true identity, asked, "What's your racket, anyway?"

"He was just using a common expression, but it made Nelson angry," Ed Burgle said. "He told my father, 'You just shut your mouth and don't say anything,' and left." Nelson then walked over to Hitchcock's dealership and bought the Plymouth. It wasn't until later that Gene Burgle learned that the "James Rogers" who left his business in a huff really was Nelson, a trigger-happy killer and bank robber.

"Fatso" Negri told the FBI that he had first met Tobe Williams in a San Francisco saloon and "had heard that he was alright and had a large political pull in Vallejo." In the FBI interview, Negri added that Williams ensured his gangster friends that he would be tipped off "within a few minutes" any time that federal agents were in town. Negri also said that during some of his numerous stops at the hospital he had met and talked with Nelson.

On one visit he saw Williams give Nelson, who needed money, $1,000 in cash from a tin box he kept on a bookcase shelf in his quarters at the hospital. Negri said he gathered that Nelson had left $5,000 with Williams, with the understanding that the money would go to Nelson's mother should something happen to him. He also told the FBI that he made several trips to the Vallejo hospital to visit Helen Nelson while she was a patient there, and brought her flowers on one of the visits. He also described a meeting with Nelson in the alley behind the hospital. Nelson, Negri said, "had a lot of money which he was counting out in piles on the back seat of his automobile. He passed me over about $300."

Williams also was questioned by FBI agents in mid-January, 1935, prior to his trial. A summary of three sessions conducted over as many days states, "It was obvious in interviewing Tobe Williams that he planned to be open about the fact that Nelson had been at the Vallejo General Hospital on the occasions noted by Negri, but that his defense would be that he did not know Nelson's identity until after Nelson was killed. It was also obvious from this interview with Williams that he had intimate knowledge of, and contacts with, the underworld in this and other parts of the United States."

"He advised that he had known, and was intimately acquainted with Bill Graham, and Jim McKay, of Reno, Nevada, James Griffin, San Francisco café owner, Ralph Rizzo, San Francisco bail bond broker, Joe Parente, San Francisco ex-bootlegger, Louis Parente, San Francisco and El Verano resort owner, and Tex Hall, manager for Graham and McKay, Reno, Nevada. He reiterated that he had first met Lester M. Gillis, alias 'Baby Face' Nelson, alias Jimmy Burnett, at Reno, Nevada, about three years ago, when his wife, Helen Gillis, alias Helen Burnett, had been with him." The report also states that Nelson, while driving one of Parente's booze trucks, "on numerous occasions ... would stop by the hospital, parking the whiskey truck in the alley behind the hospital, and coming into the hospital to use the telephone."

In an April 9, 1935, *Woodland Daily Democrat* account published following Williams' harboring conviction, he was described as "a small town Dr. Jekyll and Mr. Hyde. By day, a philanthropist, a humanitarian. By night the confidante and confrere of America's 'big time' crooks. That is the picture Vallejo sees today—and gasps at." At Vallejo General Hospital, the newspaper said, "no poor family who appealed to him for help was ever turned away. No down-and-outer was ever refused aid." Despite rumors about "the strange doings" at his hospital, Williams remained "the prominent Vallejo business man and politician," the *Daily Democrat* said, adding, "Then came the blast that rocked this peaceful community. The Department of Justice 'got wise.' The 'G' men uncovered records of Big Tobe's dual life, and he was shaken from the fringe of the underworld into the cell of a federal prison."

After his release from prison, the elderly Williams returned to his post as general manager of his hospital. The hospital was also his home. His quarters consisted of his office and an adjoining room with a bed and shower bath. FBI agents who inspected the room noted that it was decorated with photographs of his friend Jack Dempsey and other fighters and sporting characters. When Williams died on July 7, 1942, at age 80 after a

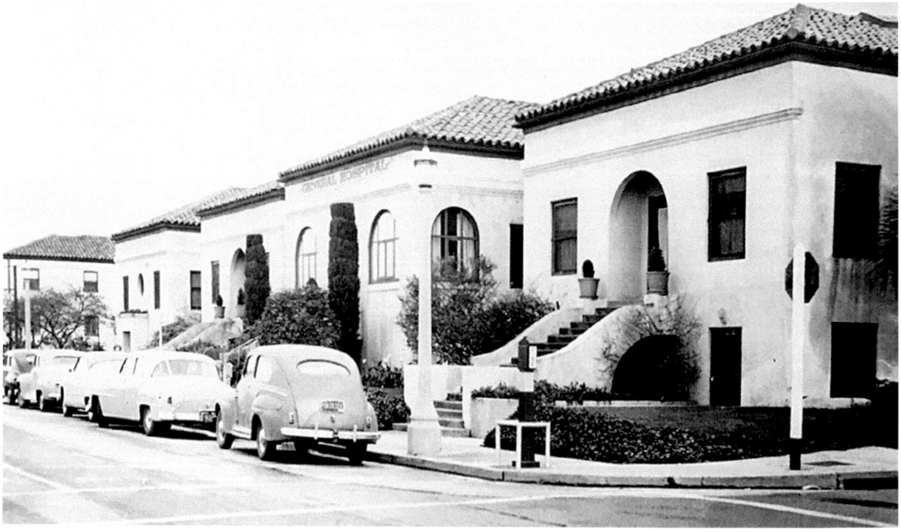

Vallejo General Hospital served Vallejo for many years. It was run by "Tobe" Williams, who led a double life as a respected hospital administrator and associate of many gangsters.*[Vallejo Naval and Historical Museum]*

protracted illness, many Vallejoans came to his funeral to pay their respects. Nurses from his hospital, all in uniform, attended the service. Newspaper obituaries made only brief mention of his past gangland connections.

As for "Baby Face" Nelson, the notorious bank robber and killer became Public Enemy No. 1 following the death of one of his crime partners, John Dillinger, in a July 22, 1934, FBI ambush. After leaving Vallejo in early October, Nelson went to Nevada and then headed for the Midwest. He died following a Nov. 27, 1934, shootout with the FBI in Barrington, Illinois His bullet-riddled body, wrapped in a blanket by Helen, was found the next day in a ditch near a cemetery in the Skokie, Illinois, area. He died ten days shy of his 26th birthday. The 5'4" gangster whose murder victims included three FBI agents—two of them at Barrington—was described by *Public Enemies* author Burrough as "the most violent of the Depression-era outlaws, a manic multiple murderer who drew disdain even as Dillinger and Pretty Boy Floyd attained the status of folk heroes. At his worst Nelson was a caricature of the public enemy, a callous, wild-eyed machine-gunner who actually laughed as he sprayed bullets toward women and children in at least two of his robberies. Nelson's behavior was so clichéd that is was as if he were acting out scenes from a gangster movie, perhaps Jimmy Cagney's 1931 hit *Public Enemy*." Nelson, born Lester Joseph Gillis, was buried in the Gillis family plot at St. Joseph's Cemetery, in River Grove, Illinois. Helen Gillis spent a year behind bars and was then granted probation. In 1937 she returned to Chicago and spent decades shunning publicity. She died in 1987 and was buried beside her husband at St. Joseph's Cemetery.

5

Concluding the 1930s, Closing in on World War II

Besides the buzz around Vallejo about "Baby Face" Nelson and other gangsters spending time in the town during the Prohibition era, the years between the end of Prohibition and the start of World War II produced Lower Georgia-related news stories that ranged from limits on drinking hours and the all-too-familiar gambling and prostitution offenses to more serious crimes such as a knifing attack and the beating death of a former sailor by several sailors. The district remained busy because Mare Island was able to slowly add employees even during the Great Depression, which lasted from 1929 to 1939—the deepest and longest economic downturn in the history of the Western industrialized world. In a 1983 *Vallejo Times-Herald* column describing how Vallejo survived the Depression with relative ease, local historian Ernie Wichels said the city was "fortunate" because of the shipyard activity. While economic hard times, coupled with a drought in the country's midsection, were prevalent elsewhere, he noted Vallejo was one of a handful of cities in the country where bank deposits increased. With more shipyard employees, more Vallejo homes were needed, and contractors were busy developing new neighborhoods.

Prohibition was over but Vallejo officials didn't want round-the-clock drinking in town. A front-page story in the Aug. 20, 1934, *Vallejo Evening Chronicle* described a city council decision to ban the sale of liquor between the hours of 1 a.m. and 6 a.m. Mayor Fred Heegler said the limit was needed to correct a condition that was "worse than the Barbary Coast at its worst." The rules also restricted waitresses to serving drinks to customers "in bona fide restaurants at tables while eating," and barred women from serving liquor at counters or bars. Police Commissioner E. J. Blanco, describing "deplorable conditions in the first and second blocks of Georgia, asserted that 63 girls are employed as barmaids in 21 licensed sandwich shops. He told of complaints from citizens and declared the time had come for city regulation," the *Evening Chronicle* said.

Police also cracked down again on illegal gambling. At 128 Georgia St., Fred Fong was arrested and charged with "conducting a gambling game behind barred doors," according to a Dec. 7, 1934, news story. And next door at a 136 Georgia St. laundry, the same article mentioned that Mary Yow was fined $50 for conducting a lottery.

The arrest of Lee Wong at a 125 Georgia St. grocery store, for conducting a lottery, was reported on March 24, 1936. And Mary Yow was arrested again, according to a Jan. 14, 1936, news story, for conducting a lottery game at 133 Georgia St. That raid also resulted in the arrests of Ed Holden for running a crap game and of well-known Lower Georgia figures George Canon and Tommy Kilbane for operating a Chinese bean game, also known as fan-tan, at the same address. Canon, described in an *Oakland Tribune* article as one of the San Francisco Bay area's "gambling kings," also had been arrested the previous September in a raid at a Port Chicago pool hall that was set up for slot machines, craps and blackjack. A raid at the Far Eastern, at 417 Santa Clara St., reported Oct. 29, 1937, resulted in four arrests on various gambling charges, including operation of a blackjack game and a lottery. A Dec. 27, 1940, report described the arrests of Gene Morgan for running a dice game at the Rex Club, 215 Georgia St., and of Riley Garling for operating a blackjack game at Dopey Norman's, 124 Georgia St.

The *Vallejo Times-Herald* urged authorities to continue the battle against illegal gambling, saying, "It is high time that Vallejo was made a safe community for the people who reside here: safe for families, safe for children. Too many husbands and fathers have been losing their pay checks in these illegal gambling houses. Lotteries and gambling games of various kinds have been allowed to run wide open, and legitimate business and family happiness have suffered."

The *Santa Cruz Evening News* joined in the pressure, stating in an Aug. 21, 1936, editorial that legitimate businesses shouldn't defend gambling "as a necessary evil." The newspaper added, "How little most of these business men know about the syndicated nature of the gambling business in California, and what pitiful examples these gambling bosses make out of public officials as they rake in their profits from the fools who buck the games, while the police departments cooperate in the outrage."

Fights in gambling houses and cafes led to more arrests in the Lower Georgia district. A Nov. 4, 1935, *Vallejo Evening Chronicle* story told of the arrest of Joseph Roach for stabbing Percy Ecklund in the left arm with a pocket knife after Ecklund refused to let him play in a card game at the Rex Club. The following week, a Nov. 12, 1935, story on the front page of the *Vallejo Evening Chronicle* told of murder charges being filed against Arthur Williams of Vallejo for the stabbing death of Leo Flythe, a sailor serving on the USS *Preble*, in a café. Williams claimed that he had to stab Flythe "or be stabbed myself." The victim was found on the floor of the café with an open razor in his hand. Police said the two men got into a fight because of "attentions paid" by Flythe to Williams' wife at an earlier dance.

A *Vallejo Evening Chronicle* account disclosed that five sailors serving on the USS *Pyro* were charged with murder for the Oct. 26, 1940, fatal beating of Robert G. Anderson in an alley behind the Navy YMCA on the edge of the Lower Georgia district. Four days after the attack, Anderson, a former sailor, died from a fractured skull and brain hemorrhage at the Mare Island Navy Hospital. Police were able to get enough information from witnesses to identify the suspects, who were arrested several weeks later in Honolulu, the *Pyro's* destination after leaving Mare Island. One of the suspects was on the *Pyro* while the other four had transferred to the USS *Yorktown*, also in Honolulu.

Problems with houses of ill repute continued in the Lower Georgia district. A May 25, 1937, news story told of a $200 fine being imposed on Mildred Adkins for "keeping a disorderly house." A March 22, 1940, news account described the arrests of two rooming-house operators, Susie Carter of 101A Georgia St. and Ann Boyd of 216A Georgia St., on the same charges. An Oct. 11, 1940, news account told of the arrests of another rooming-house operator, Amber Allen, for "purchasing a woman for immoral purposes" for $50. That story also named Howard Hyatt, charged with pandering for first taking the woman from San Francisco to a Benicia "resort" and then to Allen's rooming house and allegedly selling her "into a life of prostitution." Parents of the 21-year-old victim learned of the situation and went to police.

After a 36-year run, Police Chief William Stanford retired in 1936 on a $125 monthly pension, half his salary. As the longest-serving police chief in the nation at the time, he had dealt with more than his share of law enforcement work. He also had dealt with 18 Mare Island Naval Shipyard commandants as well as many prosecutors, judges, council members and mayors. His replacement, Bert Forman, was no newcomer to Vallejo. He had been hired by Stanford in 1920 and had worked his way up through the ranks. When the Police Department was reorganized starting in early 1941, another veteran lawman from Vallejo, Earl Dierking, took over as chief. Forman then became assistant chief and served in that capacity until retiring in 1954.

By 1940, Vallejo's business district had completed a gradual transition and most of the businesses in the 100 and 200 blocks of Georgia Street were bars, liquor stores, gambling houses, arcades, tattoo parlors, brothels, boarding houses and hotels. During the war years, it would be a round-the-clock scene.

City directories show, for example, that in 1917 tailor shops occupied 101 Georgia St. and 124 Georgia St. In the World War II era, bars and liquor stores were at those addresses. In the same time frame, 106 Georgia went from a general merchandise store to pawn shop and loan office; and 146 Georgia changed from a cigar shop to a liquor store. The law office at 145 Georgia was gone, replaced by a rooming house and taxi business. The grocery at 147 Georgia became a bar. Instead of the candy and ice cream shop at 236 Georgia, there was a drug store and, later, a liquor store. The wood, coal, hay, grain and feed store at 239 Georgia became a hotel and club; and the fruit and vegetable shop at 228 Georgia had also become a hotel and club.

An *Associated Press* account that ran in papers on April 30, 1941, told how Police Chief Dierking, off duty and out of uniform, was taking an evening stroll when he was invited

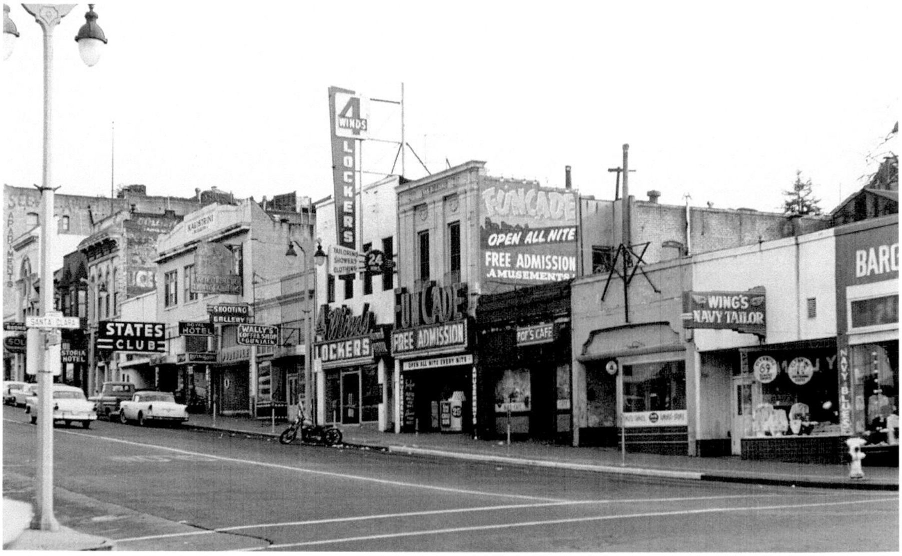

Several of the bars and other joints in the 200 block of Lower Georgia Street can be seen in this photograph taken by Tom Slaight in the early 1960s. *[Tom Slaight collection]*

into a Lower Georgia club by a doorman. "Come right into the club room, buddy—got some swell games back there," the doorman said. The offer "interested him. So he went in," the *AP* story stated. "He walked down a long hall, peeked in at a dice game, nabbed the doorman and two others in the hall, and took them to the lockup. Then he sent an inspector for the operator of the dice game." The operator wound up paying a $250 fine and the other three paid $25 fines for vagrancy.

The Nov. 7, 1941, *Vallejo Evening News* carried a front-page story of a drive by Dierking to rid Vallejo of "undesirables" following complaints by several men that they were victims of pickpockets. The account, headlined "Police Nip Baby Crime Wave," said four women with long police records for petty crime pleaded guilty in Police Court to vagrancy charges and were ordered to get out of town.

While local authorities were busy dealing with various types of crime in the Lower Georgia district just prior to the nation's entry into World War II, that was nothing compared with what was right around the corner. The problems faced by Vallejo increased as hiring ramped up at Mare Island as part of a war preparedness campaign. From a low of about 6,000 shipyard workers in early 1939, Mare Island had increased its workforce to about 12,000 by 1940 and to about 30,000 by the time that Japanese airplanes attacked Pearl Harbor on Dec. 7, 1941. Mare Island employment, ship construction and repairs and other activity climbed to record highs following the attack, changing Vallejo in ways that residents could not have imagined.

6

World War II— War Changes Everything

The Dec. 7, 1941, attack by Japan on Pearl Harbor ratcheted up activity on Mare Island and in Vallejo to a level never seen before or since. Civilian shipyard employment soared to about 44,000 during the war, with workers coming from almost every state. Sailors, Marines and Army soldiers arrived by the thousands, and Vallejo's pre-war population of about 30,000 tripled. A third of the wartime population lived in hastily constructed housing projects scattered around the city—projects that were filled as soon as they were built. About 300 buses went out in a radius of 75 miles six times a day to pick up workers who lived outside Vallejo.

In the months before Dec. 7, Mare Island had tightened security and Vallejo had turned into what the *Vallejo Times-Herald* described as "a milling, restless mass of people." Arnold Lott wrote in *A Long Line of Ships* that "For Rent" signs disappeared "and a cry arose over gouging practices of 'rent hogs.' A clamp-down on vice in defense areas got full local support. The cities had better clean up, warned California's Attorney General, Earl Warren, or the State and Federal authorities would. Strict control of visitors on Mare Island brought local realization that the situation was considered close to war."

The day after the Dec. 7 attack on Pearl Harbor, workers started pouring cement for bomb shelters on Mare Island. Soon, the shipyard was "bristling with anti-aircraft batteries" and "a herd of barrage balloons was tethered above the island, their purpose being to discourage attack by low-flying planes," Lott wrote. Security efforts included a Feb. 5, 1942, raid by about 50 FBI agents, Vallejo police and Solano County sheriff's deputies that resulted in arrests of nine "Japanese enemy aliens" in or near the Lower Georgia district, the *Vallejo Times-Herald* reported in a front-page story. The arrests were made at a laundry, a café in the 200 block of Georgia Street frequented by sailors and shipyard workers and at a nearby home. Contraband seized by the authorities included radios, cameras, two rifles, two Navy signal flags and "several suitcases full of undisclosed contraband," the newspaper said. Eleven others nabbed in the raid were released after questioning.

With the lack of adequate housing in Vallejo, some newly hired defense workers slept in cars, on porches, in hallways, bathrooms, abandoned shacks, barns, garages or on the docks. Four or five would crowd into a small hotel room. Rents for any sort of shelter soared by more than 50 percent, prompting formation on Aug. 20, 1941, of a "fair rent committee" to stop landlords from exploiting their tenants. "War was declared last night on rent profiteers in Vallejo and an eight-man board was named to wage that war," the *Times-Herald* stated the next day, adding that board members said they would be "fair and square with landlord and tenant alike—and pull no punches when they discover out-and-out cases of rent profiteering."

The committee wound up handling more than 200 cases of alleged rent-gouging, trying to resolve rent disputes or imposing fines when landlords refused to cooperate. One case involved a landlord with a house that had been rented to two families for a total of $40. The building was cut up into eight one-room apartments, each renting for $35 a month. In another case, a landlord evicted six families from a house on the pretext that he was going to remodel the place as a rooming house. In many cases, prices were adjusted to salaries. A well-known submarine commander had to pay $150 a month for one room and a bath for himself, his wife and two children.

With the Navy's massive buildup underway on Mare Island, it didn't take long for Rear Adm. Friedell, the shipyard commandant, to lay down the law with local authorities. In a Feb. 9, 1942, letter to the City Council, bannered on the front page of the *Times-Herald*, Friedell said prostitution in Vallejo brothels "has never been consistently or successfully repressed" despite multiple attempts to do so. Those attempts had been sought by the Vallejo Ministerial Union, which had launched its own anti-vice campaign a year earlier.

"In addition, the problem of women working in bars and taverns in Vallejo, ostensibly as waitresses but in reality to increase the sale of liquor and to solicit sailors, has increased alarmingly and is seriously affecting the health and efficiency of sailors frequenting these places," Friedell wrote. "In 18 bars and taverns located in two blocks on lower Georgia Street, approximately 80 women are so employed." The admiral added that local officials "are apparently indifferent and tolerant of present conditions. Commercial prostitutes have been required to have inspection slips, but 'waitresses' in bars and taverns, by mutual agreement of owners, police, and health officials, are only required to have 'food handlers' cards which in reality are statements of freedom from venereal disease."

J. Hayden Perkins, the city's commissioner of public health and safety, said the city would cooperate with the Navy but the tripling of the city's population "brings in a particular element hard to combat." Suppressing prostitution "is only one of the multitudinous duties heaped upon an already overworked police department," Perkins said, adding that the admiral's information was "compiled in a very loose and haphazard manner, more based on hearsay than any scientific fact." Perkins also said commercial prostitution was being "consistently repressed" by local authorities, but policing "barmaids and pick-ups" in restaurants wasn't the city's concern. Instead, he said it was a responsibility of the state Board of Equalization.

In a June 1, 1942, news story in the *Oakland Tribune*, a Vallejo group called the Citizen Committee of 500 said progress had been made in reducing prostitution although several houses "are still operating and others are waiting to open if local vigilance is relaxed." The committee added that gambling establishments "continue to operate with little or no interference from local authorities." Its findings were being sent to state Attorney General Earl Warren.

While the Navy and the city debated how to handle the problems in the Lower Georgia Street district, many sailors liked what they saw. One, Jimmy Albert Nagle, even wound up writing a book, *The Unholy Three*, about the adventures he and two of his shipmates had in Vallejo and elsewhere during their years in the Navy. "All you heard about Mare Island and Vallejo was how swell the liberty was," Nagle wrote. "It was supposed to be a paradise for all good seafaring men. It had bars all the way up Georgia Street, gambling in the rear, and many cathouses above."

The Lower Georgia Street district was "the best damn liberty port on the West Coast," Nagle said. "The small ferries ran night and day to the landing at the foot of Georgia Street. The bars going up Georgia Street on the starboard were Anchor, Dopey's, Owl, Three Star, Chris, Naval Base, and many more too numerous to mention. There were at least 20 taverns in the first two blocks. Some had gambling in the back and about half of them had a cathouse upstairs. It was really handy, with everything a good clean-living swab jockey could want."

"What a wonderful time we single sailors enjoyed. A water taxi was on call day or night for only one thin dime. It would drop us off at the foot of Georgia Street and bring us back, anytime," Nagle said. "Riding the ferry back we looked at Georgia Street, thinking what a wonderful place to really have a good time. If a person had never seen or been there, it would have been hard to believe such a street existed."

Hollywood even took notice of the Lower Georgia Street district, with a few lines in a popular 1942 propaganda film, *Wake Island*, starring William Bendix, Robert Preston and Brian Donlevy. In the film, Marines, about to be overrun by attacking Japanese, talk about where they'd rather be. One, portrayed by Bendix, says he'd like to be with Myrtle. Another Marine says, "Aw, no, something better than Myrtle."

Bendix asks, "What could be better than Myrtle?"

"Lots of things," the other Marine says.

"Yeah, how do you know?" asks Bendix.

"All right, I was stationed at Mare Island too," the other Marine replies.

Asked to think of something else, Bendix says, "No, it's still Myrtle."

"One-track mind," his buddy says.

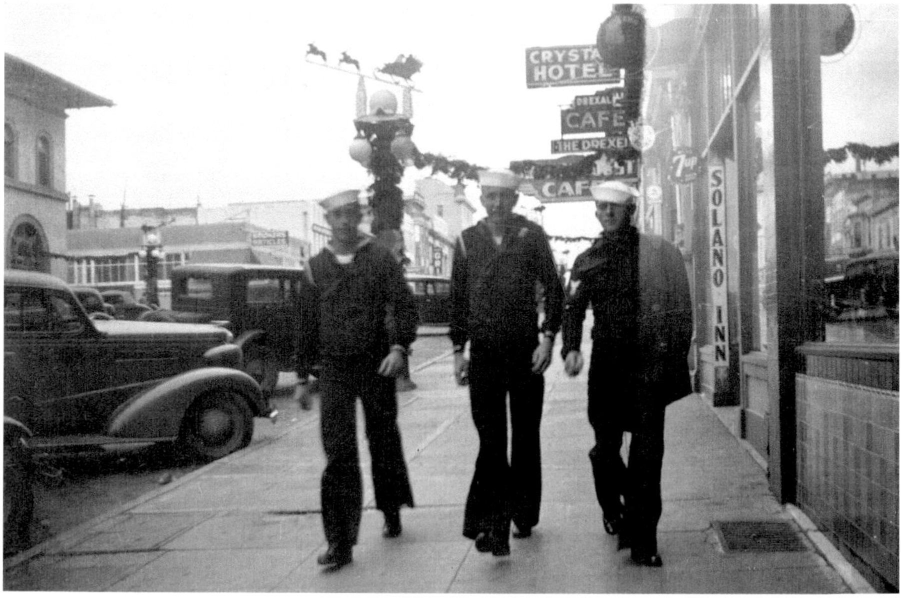

Three sailors on liberty walk down the 200 block of Georgia Street, in the Lower Georgia district. *[Tom Quinn collection]*

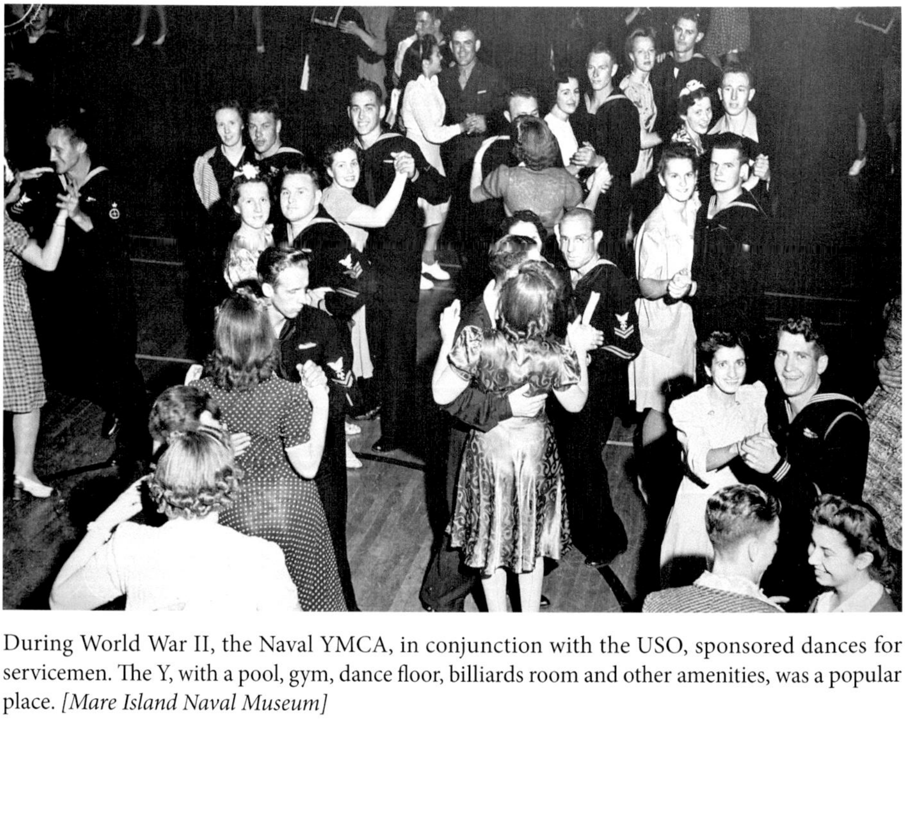

During World War II, the Naval YMCA, in conjunction with the USO, sponsored dances for servicemen. The Y, with a pool, gym, dance floor, billiards room and other amenities, was a popular place. *[Mare Island Naval Museum]*

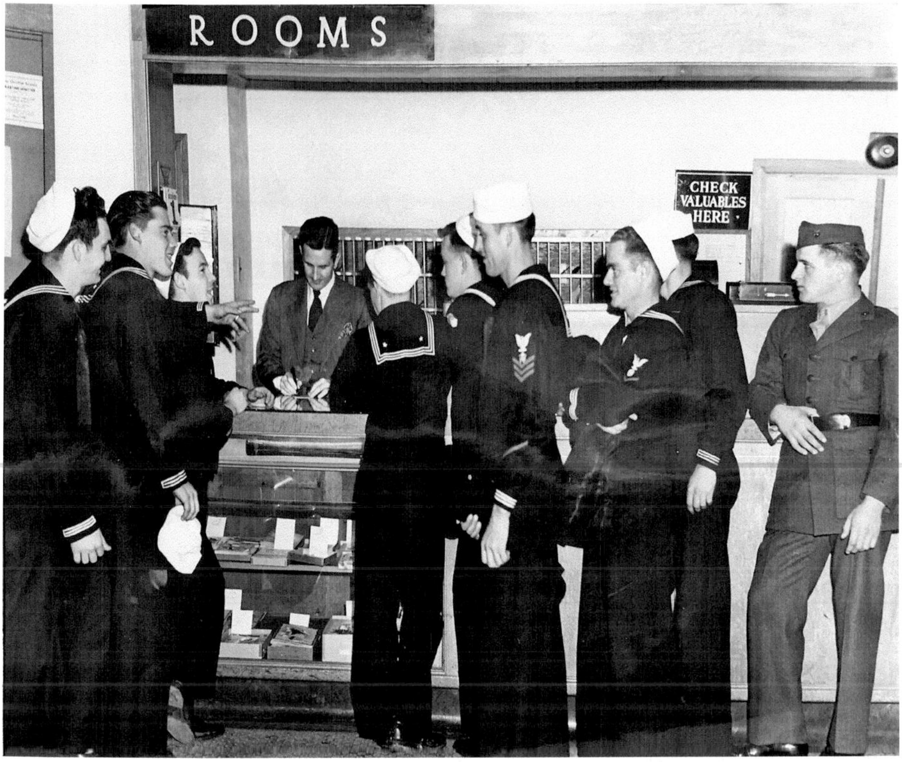

Several sailors and a lone Marine, on the right, register for rooms at the Naval YMCA near downtown Vallejo. *[Vallejo Naval and Historical Museum]*

How Locals Saw Their Town

The district was also a draw for some of the town's more adventurous young people. Joyce Georgetti, a teenager during World War II, says she was forbidden to walk around the district unless she was going to her father's small pawnshop in the 200 block of Georgia Street. She made it a point to visit his shop as often as possible. "I went down there many times, much to my father's upset," she said. "I was curious, I wanted to look it over. Lower Georgia Street was very colorful, very interesting. You knew something exciting was going on there, all the time. I mean it was wide open, it wasn't a secret about what was going on." A police officer who knew her father and whose beat covered the district would often spot her when she was headed to the pawnshop, "and he would escort me," Joyce said. "On the way down the street all these girls (in second-floor windows above the street) would lean out and wave and say hello."

"There were a lot of gambling places. I knew of about ten different places that had a gambling hall in them. My father (Harry Feinberg) always used to say that if he had a penny for every $5 he loaned to gamblers he would be a millionaire. The gamblers would pawn a lot of things. They would pawn everything to gamble," Georgetti said. "I wanted to go into one of the houses of ill repute, but dad would have killed me. He would never have approved of that. My father didn't really want me to know too much about what was going on. But it didn't really matter because I worked in the City of Paris (an upscale department store one block from Lower Georgia) and the girls from the houses used to shop there. There was one in particular I really liked. She was very pretty and had a college degree. I asked her why she was doing it (working in a brothel) and she said she was making really good money. One time when she came in we were selling Chinese robes. She bought six of them, one for her and the others for the girls she worked with."

When the war began and the Lower Georgia district was packed with servicemen, Joyce said she and her friends wouldn't date any of them. Vallejo was a tolerant town but "one thing people weren't tolerant about was dating sailors," she said. "You didn't date sailors or Marines because you got a bad reputation if you did," she said. "It was just so cruel, so unfair. They were here to help us."

If locals were avoiding sailors, there also were accounts of sailors staying out of the way of Vallejo residents walking along Georgia Street sidewalks. Terry Curtola, Vallejo's mayor from 1979 to 1987, recalls walking down Georgia Street as a young boy in the mid-1940s, holding his mother's hand. Headed to Parmisano's Fish Market, they encountered a sailor fighting a Marine outside a bar. "These two guys were punching each other out. One of them had a bloody nose. Mom just kept walking, looking straight ahead. They stopped fighting and backed away from each other so we could get by them and go to Parmisano's," Curtola said. "I looked back at them—and as soon as we had walked by they started fighting again. It was like a break between rounds in a boxing match."

Curtola also shared an example of the widespread reputation of the Lower Georgia district. While serving as vice mayor in 1973, he flew to Washington, D.C., to attend a House Armed Services Committee hearing on funding for a Carquinez Strait dredging project. The committee chair was powerful U.S. Rep. Mendel Rivers of South Carolina. Curtola, who had never testified before a congressional committee, had been coached in advance to keep his comments to a minimum given the lawmakers' busy schedules. But as soon as Rivers heard Curtola introduce himself as Vallejo's vice mayor, he interrupted him and started asking about the status of the Lower Georgia district. Rivers knew all about its colorful history. Early in his nearly 30-year career in the House, he had served on the House Naval Affairs Committee during its investigation into vice problems in Vallejo and other naval port communities. That familiarity didn't hurt. He assured Curtola and the rest of the Vallejo contingent there would be no roadblocks for the funding request. Coming from Rivers, who had recently been honored by having a nuclear submarine named after him, that was a promise the Vallejo contingent could take to the bank.

Longtime Vallejo attorney Mike Ioakimedes grew up a few blocks from the Lower Georgia district and worked with his brother in their father's grocery and liquor store, George's Grocery, at 111 Georgia St., in the heart of the district. He saw sailors going in and out of bars on the street, and shipyard workers buying half-pint bottles of liquor going to and returning from their jobs on Mare Island. Some would even take the noon ferry from the shipyard to Vallejo to buy another bottle. He says he knew about the prostitutes in nearby second-floor boarding houses, who would come into the store "and buy the good booze, the good stuff." He wasn't aware of big-time gambling or other organized crime activity but had heard hearsay accounts of "some of the local gendarmes" collecting protection money from bar owners. "When I was a kid, some of the old-timers would ask me to mark the numbers on their tickets for the lottery that was operated out of a Chinese laundry around the corner," Ioakimedes said, adding, "There's no question about the way it was. It's what you experienced. It was just part of our life."

"To me, this was a Navy town. That's how we looked at it. We had the Navy and I figured that's the way any Navy town would be. Lower Georgia was where the sailors went, period. There was a 'Ripley's Believe it or Not' story that in two blocks there were more neon signs here than anywhere else in the world. To me it was just normal. We were used to it. The bar owners were making money and the sailors were happy. If they wanted a girl, they knew where to find her. They had their place, the two blocks of Georgia Street where they hung out—not that they couldn't go further up the street if they wanted to."

Ioakimedes said he didn't see "any major problems of any kind," although he recalled a warning from military police on a Sunday in 1942 to lock up the store and go home due to the possibility of a riot. He also was working at the store on VJ Day in 1945 when military police came in again and said the store had to close. "We had to board up the windows so that people on the street wouldn't break them," he said. "The MPs said it would be a good idea since we were selling booze."

Dennis Sullivan was a teenaged pilot for the Mare Island Ferry Co., which transported about 50,000 shipyard workers, sailors and others across the Mare Island Strait every day during World War II. When he would walk from his home to the ferry landing, Sullivan said, "Georgia Street would be covered with people, and so would the alleys. There were more bars than you could shake a stick at. On top of just about every bar there was a house of ill repute."

In 1950, Sullivan hired on as a city policeman, and one of his first beats was the Lower Georgia district. "When the war was over everything went downhill, went to hell on Lower Georgia. It was different, just different," he said. "When Jack Stiltz got in as police chief, his first job was to clean up Lower Georgia, and that's what he did. But closing it down wasn't done overnight. It took a few years." Sullivan recalled situations on Lower Georgia involving "sailors lined up on one side of the street and Marines on the other. They'd be drunk and get into a tiff. But then they'd calm down." When working undercover, in efforts to shut down whorehouses, Sullivan told of "a place on Santa Clara Street run by a woman named Mary. She had just one girl working for her. When we arrested the girl, Mary said she was the best one she ever had, she would turn 50 tricks a night. After that, Mary got arrested too. After I arrested her girl, she started turning tricks herself."

The stories told about the district circulated for years among sailors and Marines who had walked along Georgia Street or had heard about it. Eric Raahauge, whose family ran the Mare Island Ferry Co. for many years, recalled hearing his brother Rob describe a conversation he had in Korea, while stationed there as a Marine in the early 1960s: "Rob and another Marine were talking about some of the crazy places they knew about, and the other guy kept talking about some town called Lower Georgia, just north of San Francisco," Eric said. "Rob finally told him that was just a street name and there was no town by that name, that he had been in Vallejo. But the guy wouldn't believe him. He was certain the town he had heard about was Lower Georgia."

While in the Navy and serving on the USS *Haleakala* in 1969, I had what normally would have been a very brief conversation with an older crew member, a usually grumpy chief, during a Pacific Ocean crossing. The ship was headed home from Vietnam, and one of our first scheduled stops was the ammunition depot on Mare Island, to unload our cargo of bombs. When I said the ship would be tying up just across the river from my hometown of Vallejo, the grouchy chief got a big smile on his face and began telling stories about the wild times on Georgia Street that he had as a young sailor in the late 1940s and early 1950s. We were always on good terms after that—I was that guy from one of his all-time favorite liberty ports.

In the early 1960s, as the city of Vallejo was moving ahead with the massive redevelopment project that resulted in demolition of the entire Lower Georgia Street district, local artist Dorothy made drawings and paintings of most of the buildings that were about to be bulldozed. This art work is the most complete record of the district, with details ranging from addresses on windows and doors to television antennas on rooftops. In the following series of drawings, you can see what sailors encountered as they walked up Georgia Street after getting off ferry boats that carried them from Mare Island to Vallejo.

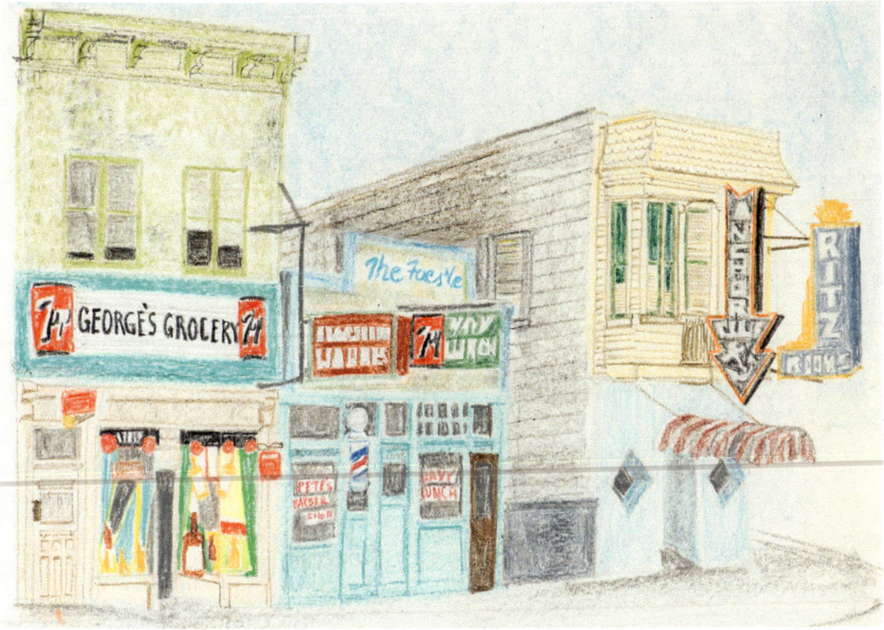

South side, 101-111 Georgia: Ritz Rooms, Anchor Club, Focs'le, Navy Lunch, Pete's Barber Shop, George's Grocery. *[Artist Dorothy Herger]*

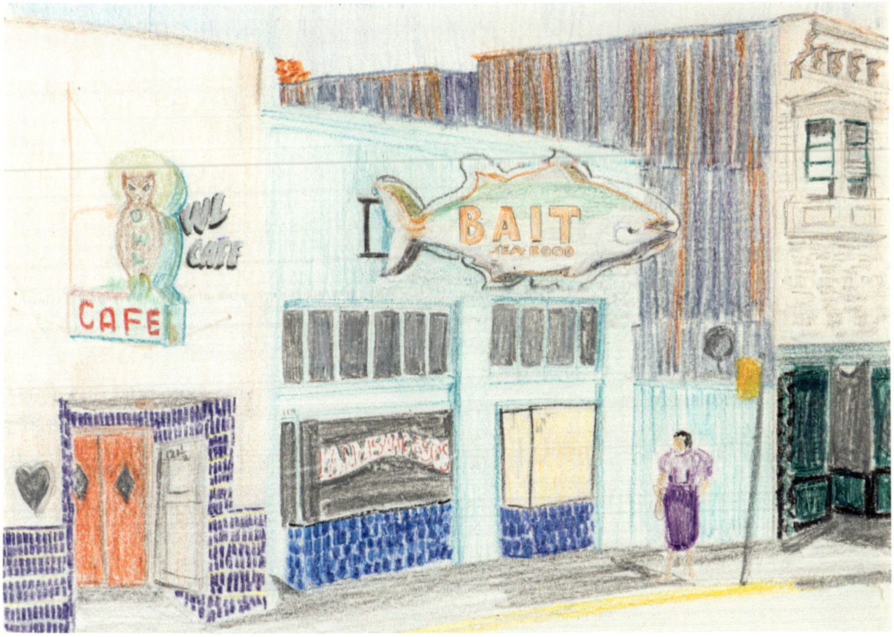

South side, 119-121 Georgia: Parmisano & Sons Fish Market, Owl Café. *[Artist Dorothy Herger]*

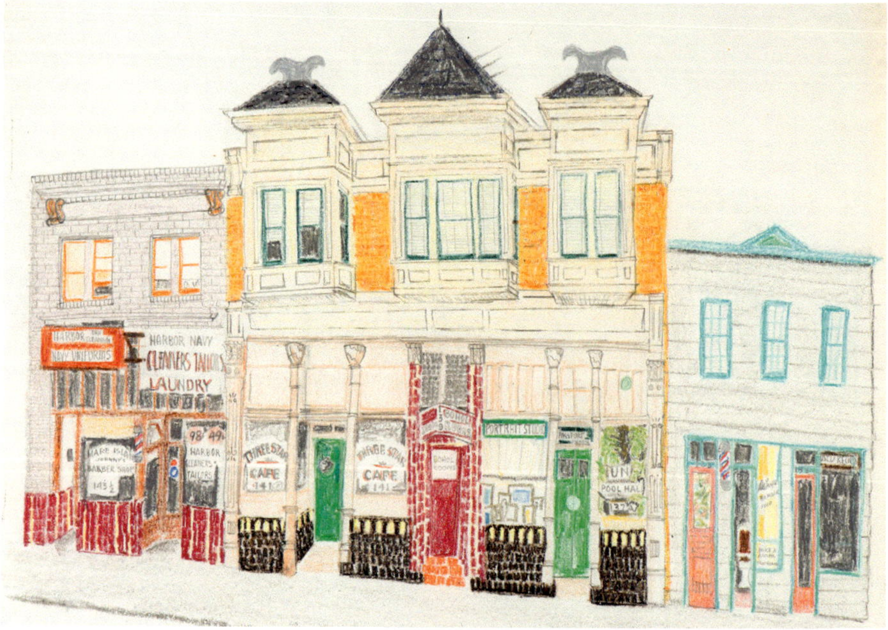

South side, 133-143 Georgia: Used records, UN Pool Hall, Deluxe Barber, Bohol Rooms, Three Star Café, Harbor Cleaners-Tailors, Mare Island Johnny's Barber Shop. *[Artist Dorothy Herger]*

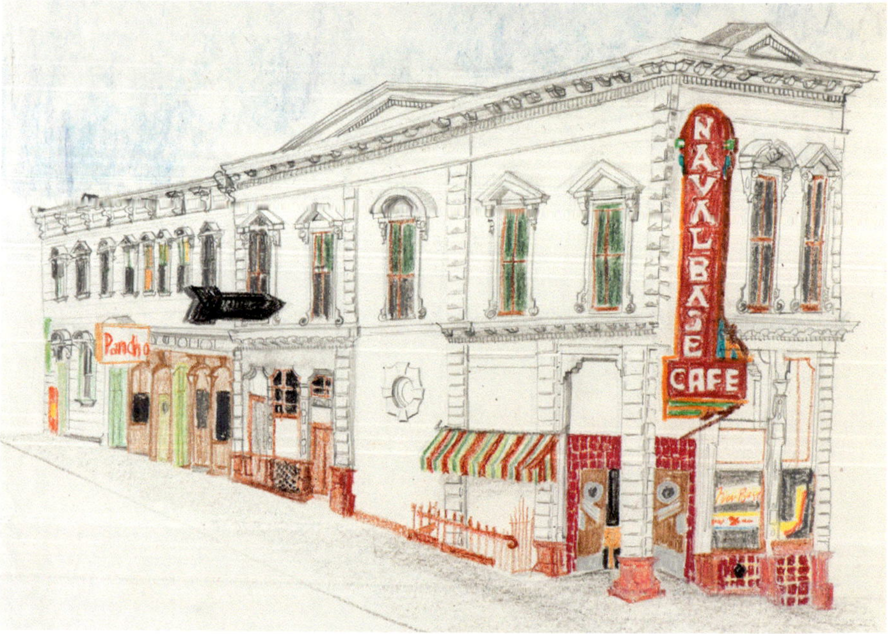

South side, 147 Georgia: Naval Base Café. *[Artist Dorothy Herger]*

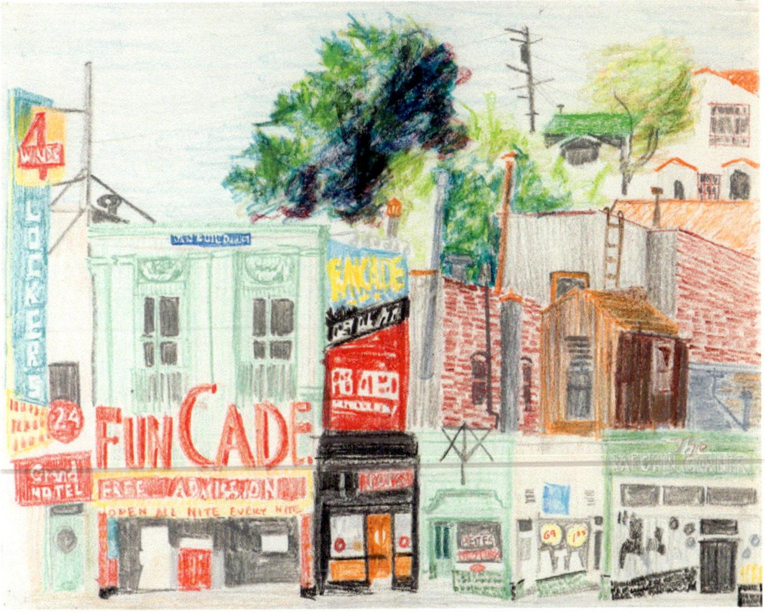

South side, 201-213 Georgia: Funcade, Grand Hotel, 4 Winds Lockers. *[Artist Dorothy Herger]*

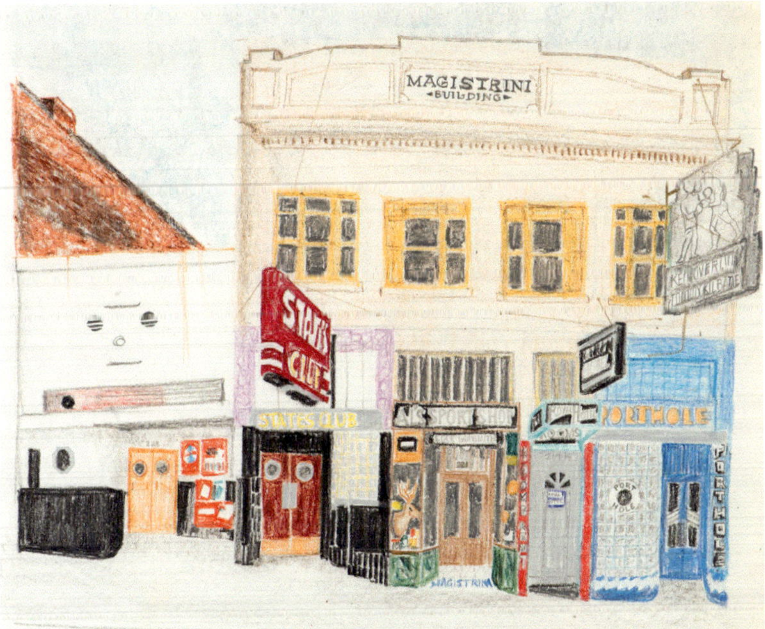

South side, 219-223 Georgia: Porthole Café, Royal Hotel, Al's Sport Shop, States Club. *[Artist Dorothy Herger]*

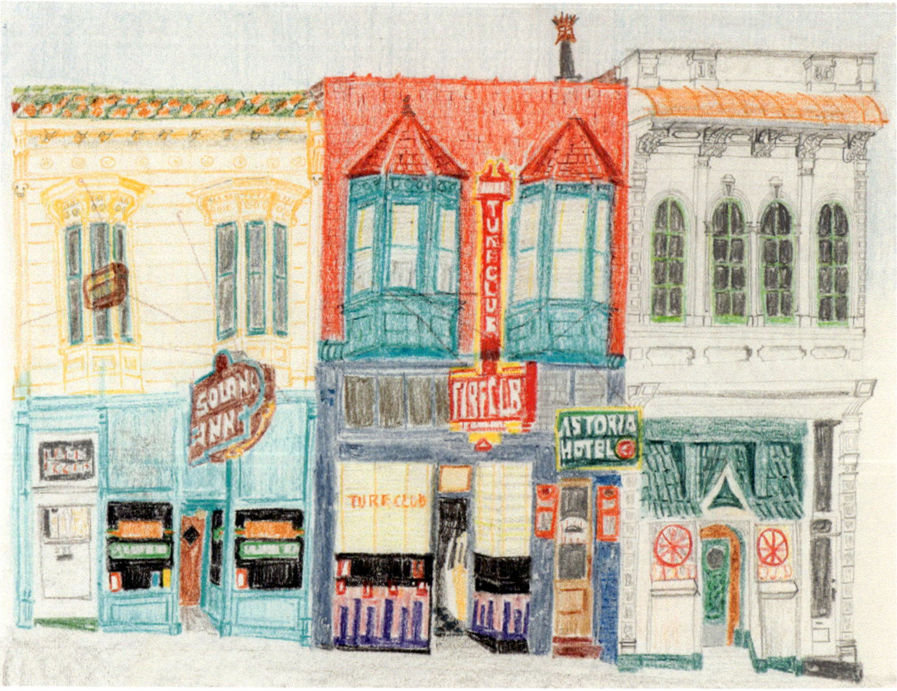

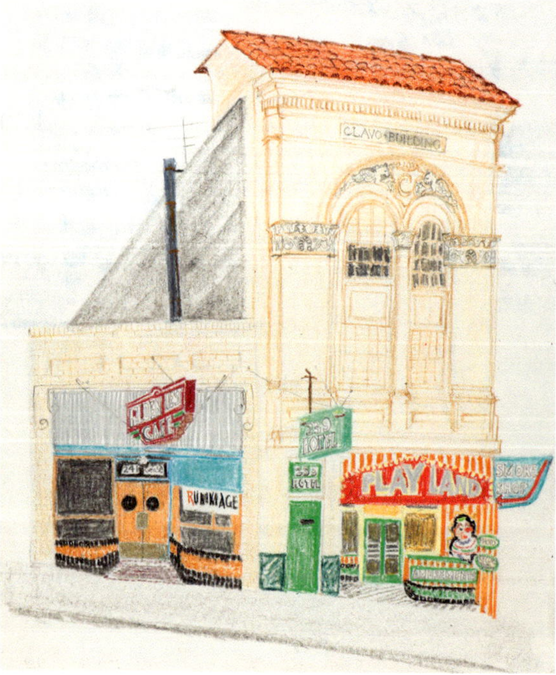

Above: South side, 229-235 Georgia: Astoria Hotel, Turf Club, Solano Inn, Lark Rooms. *[Artist Dorothy Herger]*

Left: South side, 237-241 Georgia: Playland, 239 Hotel, Golden West Café. *[Artist Dorothy Herger]*

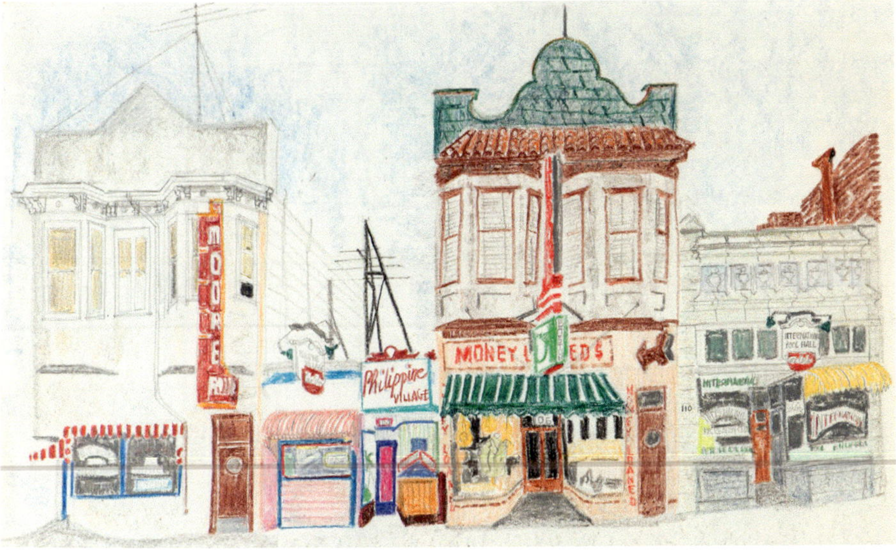

North side, 102-110 Georgia: Moore Rooms, E. Cook's Shine Parlor, Philippine Village, Boston Loans, Portland Hotel, International Pool Hall. *[Artist Dorothy Herger]*

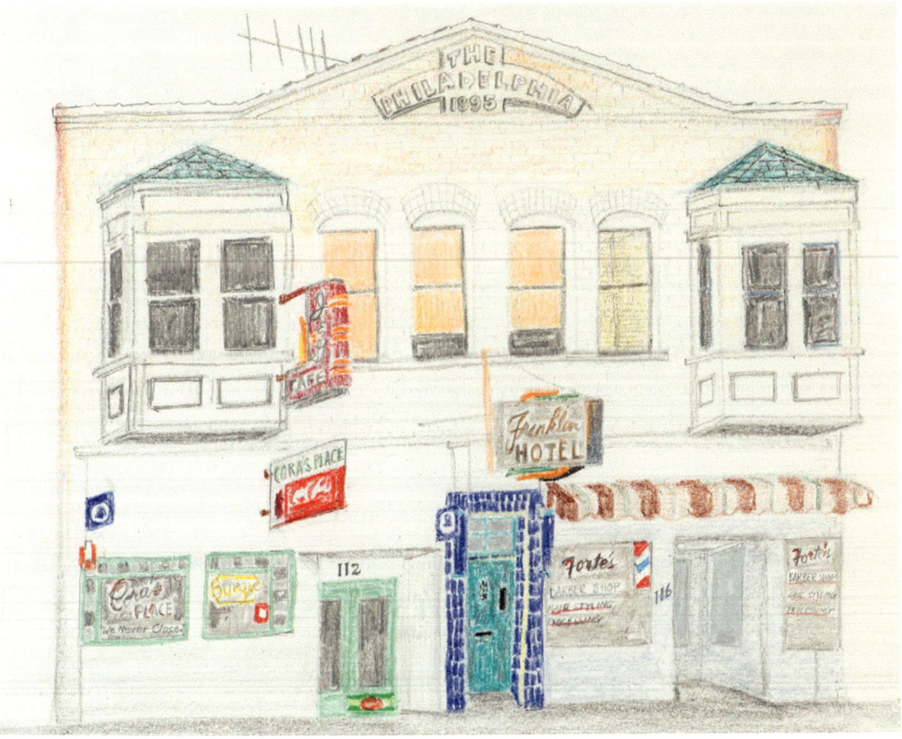

North side, 112-116 Georgia: Cora's Place, Franklin Hotel, Forte's Barber Shop. *[Artist Dorothy Herger]*

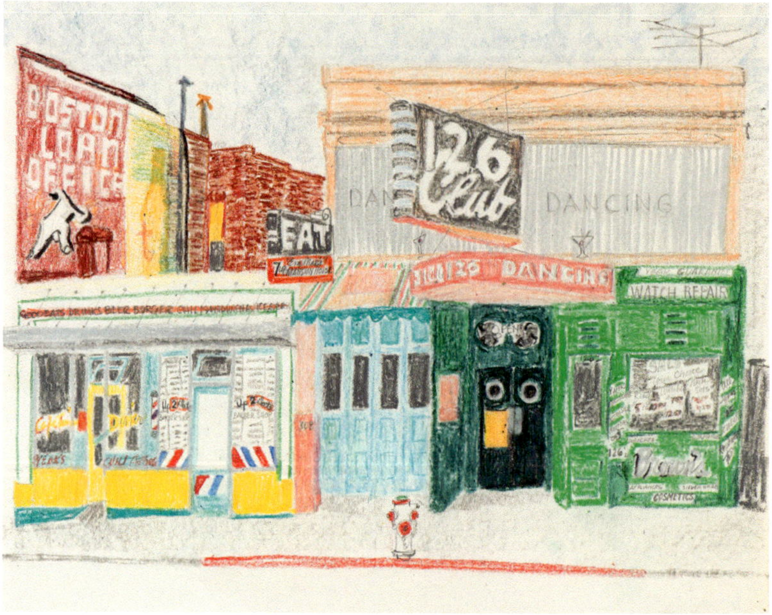

North side, 122-126 Georgia: Cafeteria/Diner, Up 2 Date Barber Shop, Eva Mae's Mansion House, 126 Club, Brown's Watch Repair. *[Artist Dorothy Herger]*

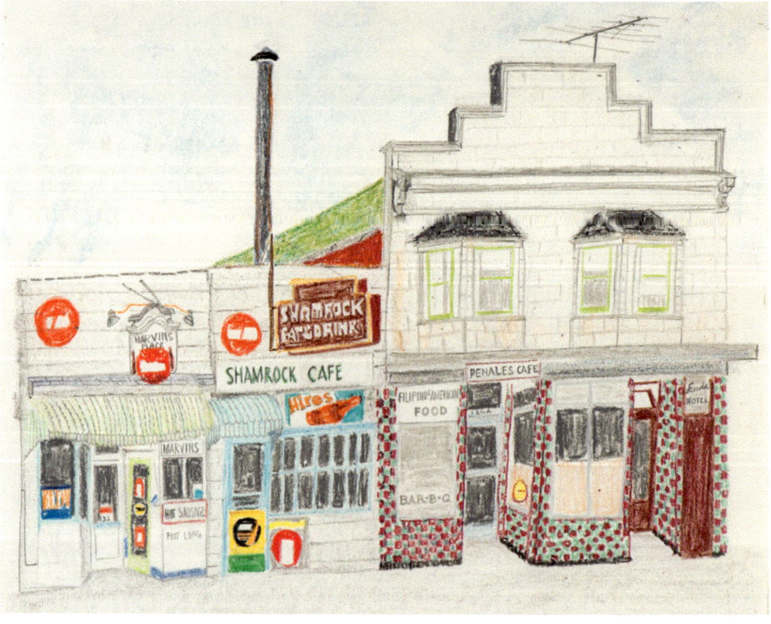

North side, 134-136 Georgia: Marvin's Place, Shamrock Café, Penales Café, Senda Hotel. *[Artist Dorothy Herger]*

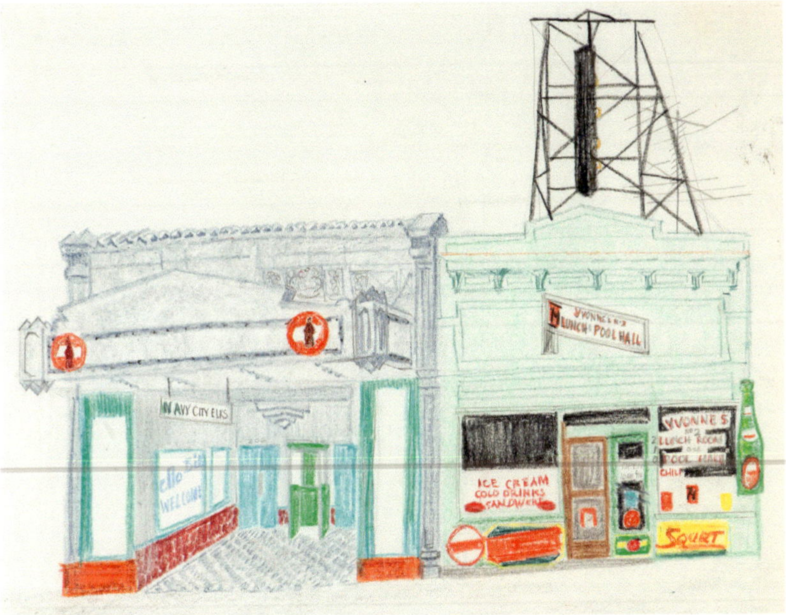

North side, 206-210 Georgia: Navy City Elks, Yvonne's Lunch and Pool Hall. *[Artist Dorothy Herger]*

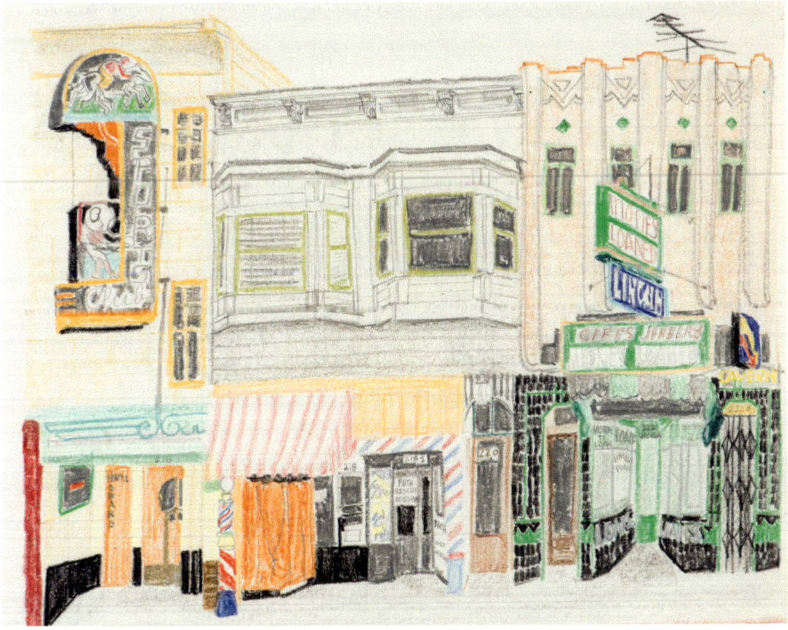

North side, 216-222 Georgia: Sports Club, barber, Howard Hotel, Faith Rescue Mission, Shasta Rooms, Lincoln Loans, Cavern. *[Artist Dorothy Herger]*

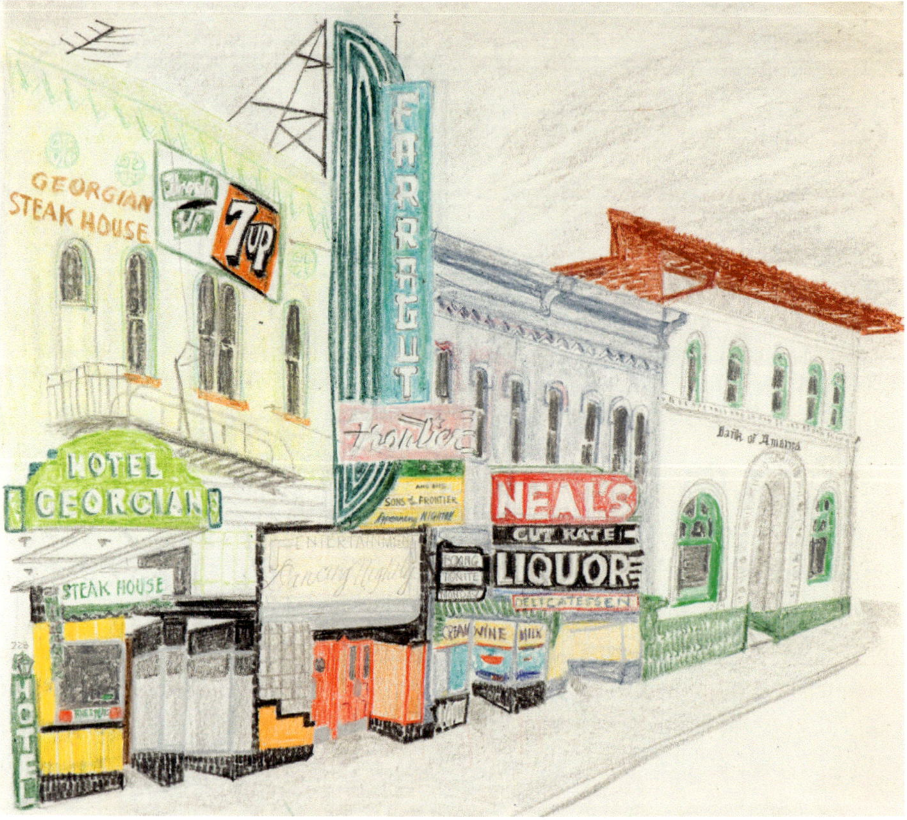

North side, 228-242 Georgia: Hotel Georgian, Neal's Liquors, Sports Arena, Farragut Club, Bank of America. [*Artist Dorothy Herger*]

7

Race Riots, Ship Explosions, Major Navy Reforms

There are some aspects of Vallejo's history that had good beginnings but bad endings, such as the gradual deterioration of Vallejo's original, thriving business district on Georgia Street into streets lined with bars, bordellos and gambling joints. But there were some bad incidents in the district that eventually figured in good, or at least improved, outcomes that spread throughout the U.S. military. At its World War II peak as a sailors' hangout, the Lower Georgia district turned into a battleground involving hundreds of sailors, Marines and civilians. The bloody rioting in late 1942 and early 1943 was triggered by segregationist policies and practices in the Navy and racism in Vallejo. The riots were followed by a horrific explosion at the nearby Port Chicago ammunition depot that killed 320 men, 202 of them black sailors who hoped for shipboard duty during the war but instead got the dangerous job of stateside ammunition-handling. Surviving black sailors were sent to segregated barracks in Vallejo. When ordered to continue loading bombs at Mare Island Naval Shipyard, many of them refused to go to the shipyard's ammunition depot. Fifty of the sailors were tried for mutiny—the largest such trial in U.S. Navy history—and received long prison sentences. But as the war drew to a close, public pressure and pleas for leniency, including one from First Lady Eleanor Roosevelt, led to reduced sentences and to an official scrapping of longstanding segregationist policies in the Navy and other branches of the military.

In *The Port Chicago 50: Disaster, Mutiny, and the Fight for Civil Rights*, author Steve Sheinkin says that as the nation raced to prepare for the war, civil rights groups challenged the Navy to abolish its racial restrictions. However, Secretary of the Navy Frank Knox insisted there was nothing he could do. "True, there was an obvious contradiction in a nation fighting for freedom while denying it to its own citizens in the military," Sheinkin says. "But, Secretary Knox explained, segregation and racism were deeply rooted facts of life in American society. These problems were not created by the military and were not the military's problems to solve."

"Aboard ships, men were crammed into close quarters, making it impossible to keep the races segregated. Neither could they be integrated, Knox argued, because white sailors wouldn't work well with black sailors, and certainly wouldn't take commands from them. To desegregate the Navy, therefore, would hurt the war effort. Knox concluded the only solution was to keep black men, other than those working as servants, off ships. The secretary insisted he was not a racist, simply a realist."

Sheinkin says President Roosevelt accepted Knox's logic, agreeing that this was no time to desegregate the Navy. "To go the whole way at one fell swoop," the president told Knox, "would seriously impair the general average efficiency of the Navy." But Roosevelt was also a politician. He counted on strong support from African American voters, and was getting pressured by black leaders to do something about the military's racial policies. So the president looked for a compromise.

In April 1942, Secretary Knox unveiled a policy change to ensure that black volunteers could get better training. But they'd be limited to low ranks, and they still could not serve aboard ships at sea, except as mess attendants. "In its abrupt announcement of a change of policy, the Navy department actually insults the intelligence of the Negroes it should seek to enlist," charged an editorial in the *Louisville Defender*, an African American–owned newspaper. "It is difficult not to feel disgusted at the tricky, evasive, hypocritical manner in which the Secretary of the Navy has dealt with this problem," added a scathing editorial in another black paper, the *Pittsburgh Courier*. Sheinkin says Roosevelt spoke in soaring phrases about America's battle to preserve freedom and democracy around the globe, but those ideals appeared to be missing at home. In spite of the protests, the Navy went ahead with its plan, and dissatisfaction among black sailors increased.

Just before the end of 1942, weekend rioting erupted in Vallejo following the arrival of several hundred black sailors newly assigned to Mare Island. Wire service stories that ran in papers around the country said the fighting began on a Saturday among about 75 black and white servicemen and some civilians. While at least four people suffered knife wounds, Rear Admiral W. L. Friedell said he planned no investigation. "I don't call it any riot," he said. "One or two sailors just got a little drunk." But Friedell couldn't dismiss the next night's rioting, involving more than 400 men. Military police fired tommy guns into the ground and the air to stop black sailors from marching on bars and night clubs that they had been blocked from frequenting, and two black sailors were wounded by ricochets, according to numerous newspaper reports.

"The chief cause of this trouble appears to be the fact that most of these colored sailors are from the south, and likewise most of the white sailors and civilians participating in the disorders are from the south," Police Chief Earl Dierking said. He added that the whites "resent the liberties the colored sailors are receiving in Vallejo and never miss an opportunity to lord it over colored men. The colored men, for their part, are attempting to go into areas that the whites have regarded as exclusively theirs since the colored men came here some weeks ago." The chief made no mention of the hard feelings among African-American sailors caused by the Navy's segregationist policies.

According to the *AP* and *UPI* accounts that ran in Dec. 28, 1942, newspapers, witnesses said the Sunday night rioting began when black sailors, carrying knives, clubs, brass knuckles, pieces of pipe and bottles, gathered outside the Knotty Pine, a black night club two blocks from Georgia Street, and then headed for the main bar district. While the machine guns stopped some of the sailors, others pushed past the military police and began fighting with whites who stormed out of bars in the downtown district. The brawling went on for about two hours, and dozens of people were treated for cuts and bruises. The next day, Marines and Navy police patrolled Vallejo streets to guard against another riot, and liberty for all military personnel was restricted. Tension eased a bit over the next few days, and USO dances on New Year's Eve went ahead on schedule. A *UPI* story filed on New Year's Eve noted, "At the request of the navy, 75 Negro girls will be sent to Vallejo tonight as dancing partners for Mare Island's Negro sailors, the USO reported today. The girls originally had been scheduled to attend a USO dance for Negro servicemen here (in San Francisco)."

Roy Wilkins, assistant secretary of the NAACP, was quoted in Jan. 9, 1943, accounts in the *Pittsburgh Courier* and *New York Age*, another black newspaper, as saying the

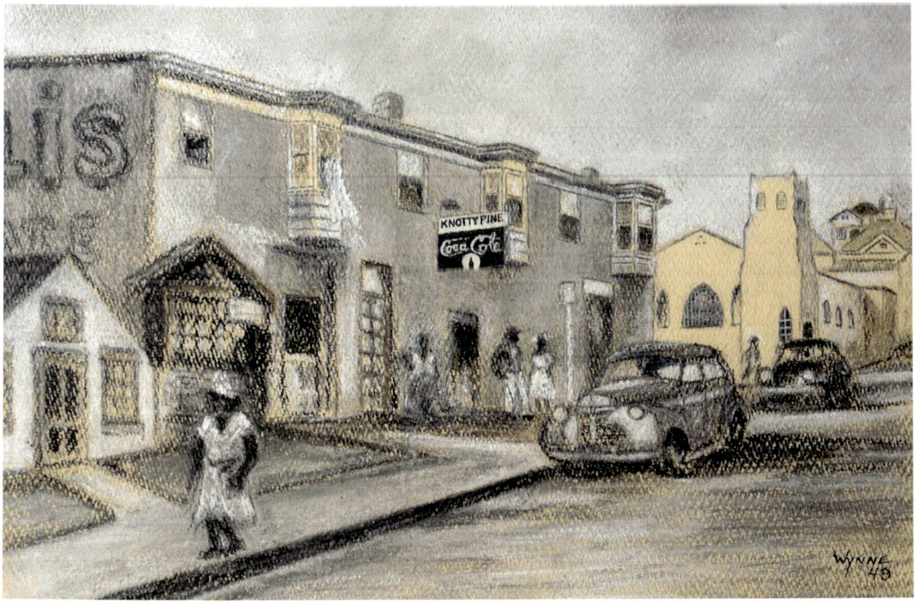

The Knotty Pine Tavern on Branciforte Street was a gathering place for African-American sailors who early in World War II were harassed by white sailors if they ventured into the Lower Georgia district only two blocks away. *[Dann Shively collection]*

outbreak in Vallejo was "in the cards" and was "no surprise" given the racial tension. "I was in Vallejo on Nov. 9, and Negro sailors who had been transferred there from the Great Lakes Naval Training Station were already bitterly complaining about the treatment they were receiving from citizens and white sailors," Wilkins stated. The *Courier* also said its correspondent overheard a desk guard say "they had killed nine Negro sailors on the second night" of the late-December rioting. No other references to sailor deaths were made in other newspaper accounts or in statements by Navy or local officials at the time. Also, a hand-written death record in the Solano County coroner's office for 1937-1946 shows no sailor deaths in Vallejo at the time of the riots. The *Courier* and the *Age* also quoted Wilkins as saying, "The heavy influx of southerners into California cannot be imagined; it has to be seen. ... There had been several minor clashes before I arrived, and the colored sailors with whom I talked were in no mood to stand much more of the insults they were receiving on every hand. Restaurants were asking them to 'take out' sandwiches. White sailors were openly testing them on the streets or beating them up if Negroes were not in a large group."

Another riot occurred on March 6, 1943, involving about 350 black and white servicemen in what a *UPI* account termed "Vallejo's Barbary Coast area." That riot, which started shortly after midnight, was broken up by about twenty Marines armed with submachine guns. Chief Dierking said a black shore patrol officer had tried to put a drunken white sailor into a taxi, but the sailor began fighting with the officer. At that point, the *UPI* story said, "servicemen poured into the street from the 200 bars in the area, taking up the fight." The crowd was too big for shore patrol and Vallejo police to handle, but the fighting stopped once the armed Marines showed up.

The large-scale rioting by sailors that occurred in Vallejo appears to be the first of its sort early in World War II. Another major incident occurred in June 1943, when over half of the 640 blacks at a Navy ammunition depot at St. Julien's Creek, Virginia, rioted against alleged discrimination. That was followed by a July protest involving 744 blacks in a construction battalion over segregation on a transport in the Caribbean.

The Port Chicago Ammunition Depot Explosion

The riots and other race-based conflicts involving Navy sailors brought attention to the Navy's segregationist polices and the need for reforms. But none of the incidents brought the segregation issues into sharper focus than the terrible July 17, 1944, explosion at the Port Chicago ammunition depot, less than 20 miles by water up the Carquinez Strait from Vallejo, that killed 320 men and injured 390 others. African-Americans accounted for 202 of the men killed and 233 of the men who were injured. The huge blast destroyed two cargo ships, the *Quinault Victory* and the *E. A. Bryan*, that were tied up at a loading pier, wrecked the Navy base and damaged the nearby town of Port Chicago. Other communities in the area, including Vallejo, sustained damage from the explosion, which has been described as the worst home front disaster of World War II. Seismograph machines at the University of California at Berkeley recorded two jolts measuring 3.4 on the Richter scale. An Army Air Force copilot flying at about 9,000 feet above Port Chicago reported debris the size of a house or garage hurtling upward past his plane. A 30-foot wall of water washed over a nearby Coast Guard vessel. The *E. A. Bryan* was blown to bits. Very little of its wreckage could be identified. The *Quinault Victory* was lifted out of the water, turned around and broken into pieces. Both ships were about 440 feet in length. The explosive force of the blast was equivalent to five kilotons of TNT, on the same order of magnitude as the atomic bomb that was dropped on Hiroshima just over a year later. After a naval court of inquiry, a judge advocate found no clear cause for the blast but listed possible factors such as detonation of some "supersensitive element, rough handling of bombs or failure of equipment." While there was no evidence of sabotage, "it cannot be ignored as a possibility," the judge advocate said.

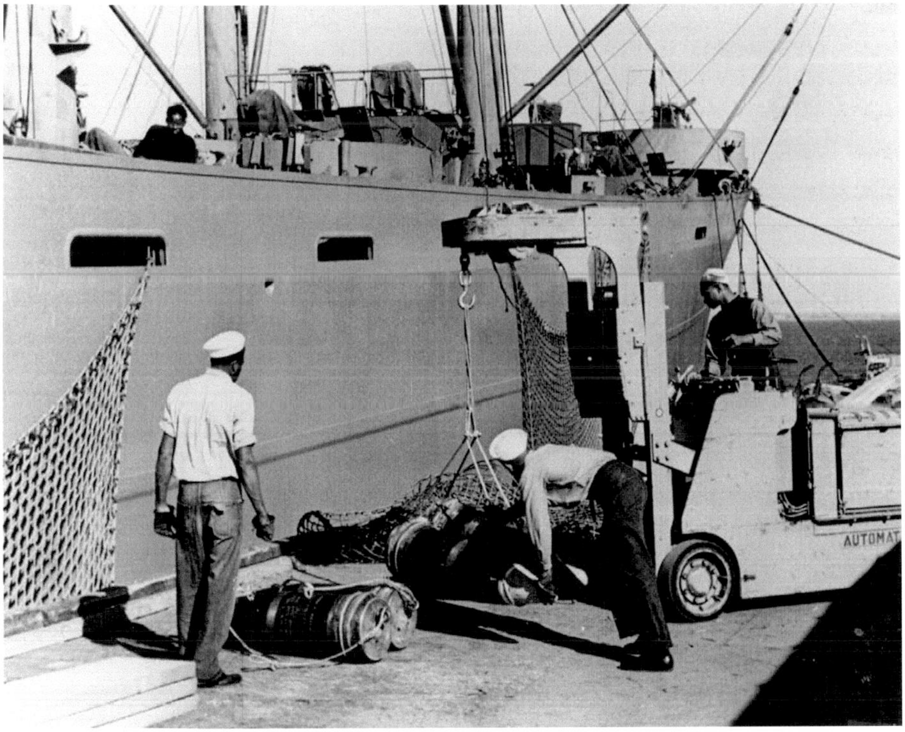

African-American sailors load ammunition at the Navy's Port Chicago ammunition depot during World War II. *[U. S. Navy/National Park Service]*

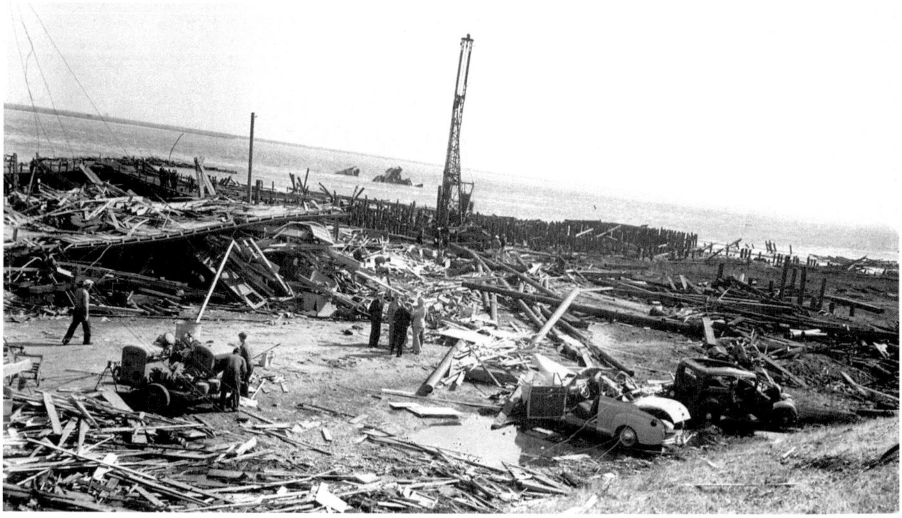

A massive ammunition explosion at the Navy's Port Chicago ammunition depot killed more than 300 sailors, two-thirds of them African-Americans, and destroyed two ships. *[U. S. Navy/National Park Service]*

On July 31, black sailors who survived the explosion were transferred to the Navy's segregated Ryder Street barracks in Vallejo, across the Napa River from Mare Island Naval Shipyard and about eight blocks from the Lower Georgia district. "It was now clear that there would be no transfer to other work, as some had hoped; there would be no 30-day survivors' leaves; the men were going to be sent back to loading ammunition under the same officers as before," Robert Allen wrote in *The Port Chicago Mutiny.* "Fearful of another explosion, angry at the treatment accorded them, the men began talking of not going back to work. For many, the risk of another explosion was uppermost in their minds." On Aug. 9, they were ordered to march toward a ferry that would take them across the river to the Mare Island ammunition depot to load bombs onto a ship, and 258 of the 328 men wound up being confined to a barge after refusing to go to work. A Navy admiral told the sailors that mutiny in time of war carried a death sentence, but Allen said 50 "refused to be cowed" and in early September were charged with conspiring to mutiny. The trial took 32 days of hearings and generated more than 1,400 pages of transcript. On Oct. 24, after only eight minutes of deliberation, the military court found all 50 defendants guilty. Each man was sentenced to fifteen years in prison. A few weeks later, the sentences were reviewed and 40 were reduced to prison time ranging from eight to twelve years. But despite appeals from NAACP Legal Defense Fund lawyer Thurgood Marshall, later a U.S. Supreme Court justice, First Lady Eleanor Roosevelt and others, the convictions were upheld in mid-1945. But then, with the Japanese surrender following the atomic bombing of Hiroshima and

Nagasaki in August, the sentences were further reduced. Finally, in January 1946, 47 of the men were freed. Two others who had been in a prison hospital were released soon after that. One sailor with a bad conduct record served additional time and was then released. All eventually received honorable discharges. The sailors were among some 1,700 imprisoned servicemen who were given clemency.

Starting in late 1944, under Navy Secretary James Forrestal's guidance, steps toward desegregation were taken, Allen wrote, noting that restrictions were lifted so that commanders could assign blacks "to such activities, and in such numbers, as they see fit." Over the next year integrated crews, with the black complement limited initially to no more than ten percent, were introduced on some auxiliary vessels. Also, orders went out to limit the number of African-American sailors at ammunition depots to 30 percent of the total, in keeping with the Navy's new policy to assure "a representative cross-section of Naval personnel at all activities."

To prepare its officers for the new era of integration, the Navy, early in 1945, issued a "Guide to the Command of Negro Naval Personnel." The fifteen-page booklet stated that "the Navy accepts no theories of racial differences in inborn ability." However, the document continued, "it is recognized, of course, that Negro performance in Naval training and tasks ... has not been equal to the average performance of white personnel." Proper training, the guide advised, could overcome the "handicaps" under which Negroes labored. Blacks were to be rated and promoted on the same basis as whites, and officers were warned against referring to blacks as "nigger." "The terms 'boy,' darkey,' 'coon,' 'jig,' 'uncle,' 'Negress,' and 'your people' are also resented," the booklet stated, adding that officers should not ask Negro personnel to do any tap dancing, guitar-playing, or singing of spirituals. In June 1945, the Navy announced it was discontinuing segregation in training camps and other programs.

In February 1946, just a month after the Port Chicago prisoners were released, the Navy became the first branch of the U.S. military to officially eliminate all racial barriers. "Effective immediately," stated the historic order, "all restrictions governing types of assignments for which Negro personnel are eligible are hereby lifted. Henceforth they shall be eligible for all types of assignments in all ratings in all activities and all ships of the naval service." Steve Sheinkin, in his *Port Chicago 50*, described how the Navy's decision to end segregation led to an even bigger change: Impressed by the progress being made in the Navy, President Harry Truman on July 26, 1948, issued Executive Order 9981, which reads in part:

> WHEREAS it is essential that there be maintained in the armed services of the United States the highest standards of democracy, with equality of treatment and opportunity for all those who serve in our country's defense:
> NOW THEREFORE, by virtue of the authority vested in me as President of the United States, by the Constitution and the statutes of the United States, and as Commander in Chief of the armed services, it is hereby ordered as follows:

> It is hereby declared to be the policy of the President that there shall be equality of treatment and opportunity for all persons in the armed services without regard to race, color, religion or national origin. This policy shall be put into effect as rapidly as possible, having due regard to the time required to effectuate any necessary changes without impairing efficiency or morale.

Vallejo author and historian Sharon McGriff-Payne is the daughter of Marshall McGriff, one of the black sailors sent to Mare Island in World War II and assigned to the ammunition dump on the shipyard instead of Port Chicago. His wife Bernice joined him in Vallejo and hired on as a civilian shipyard employee. "My father knew many of the sailors killed at Port Chicago," McGriff-Payne said. "Imagine your friends getting killed, and you still have to go to work and do the same exact thing that they were doing." Adding to the stress of ammunition-handling was the racial animosity within the Navy and Vallejo, but McGriff-Payne said her father came from Lake Wales, Florida, and was "accustomed to racism. When black people came here in World War II, they didn't think they were escaping racism. But on the other hand, this was better than back in the South. People made a little more money, and my father said that what he liked was that he didn't have to say 'Yes sir' and 'No sir' to white people." After McGriff got out of the Navy at the end of the war, the family returned to Florida for a few years, but then returned to Vallejo and stayed. McGriff returned to civilian life, working in construction and trucking, and wasn't in the Navy as desegregation began to slowly take effect. But McGriff-Payne said an uncle was able to benefit from the changes in the military in the early 1950s, serving in a partially integrated Marine Corps unit in Korea.

8

THE WAR YEARS AND THE WILD YEARS

IN EARLY 1943 a congressional panel announced that several naval port communities would be investigated because of "vice conditions," and Vallejo was on the list. The *Vallejo Evening Chronicle* reported on Feb. 23, 1943, that the House Naval Affairs Committee had called for the probe into "the situation created by war-expanded populations and naval activity" in and around Vallejo and other San Francisco Bay area port communities. Also on the list were San Diego, California; Portsmouth, Maine; Newport, Rhode Island; and Norfolk, Virginia. That was followed by Navy demands for a prostitution cleanup in Vallejo and moves in May, June and October 1943 by the Federal Security Agency to stop "commercialized prostitution." Vallejo police joined in the effort, which included raids reported in the Oct. 13, 1943, *Vallejo Times-Herald* that led to the arrests of 27 alleged madams and prostitutes. FSA representative Stewart Stimmel told the Vallejo City Council that the federal government was moving against prostitution "purely on the basis of the welfare and health of the armed forces and war workers, and that the moral question of promiscuous association was not involved," the *Times-Herald* said. Controlled brothel districts do little to control venereal disease, Stimmel said, adding that when brothel operators are shut down "there is a tendency on the part of the individuals to wait until the heat is off, that the police are less vigilant, and then reopen. The same establishments operate time and time again, despite repeated warnings by police and the FSA." Stimmel also said that when brothels are open, there's typically an effort to lure local women into the brothels "because these places thrive on change."

At the same City Council meeting, Sheriff Jack Thornton reported that the women's ward at the county jail was designed for no more than ten inmates but at times was crowded with two dozen women, many of them with venereal diseases. Council members also were asked by Police Chief Dierking to revoke the licenses for rooming houses at 413 Santa Clara St., Belva Rooms at 136C Georgia St., Moore Rooms at 102 Georgia, the Franklin Hotel at 114 Georgia St., the Grand Hotel at 213 Georgia St. and the Crystal Hotel at 239 Georgia St. The police chief said the licenses were held by women who had forfeited bail on vice charges.

Bob Louie, who operated the Navy Shell service station on the corner of Georgia and Branciforte streets, across the street from Moore Rooms, described the brothel madam, a woman named Dorothy, as a big tipper. Louie said Dorothy gave a $5 tip every time she came in for fuel, an oil change or any other service for her car. "Everyone working in the station wanted to help her," Louie said. "So we had a rule that we had to take turns when she drove in." Louie added that the service station's business was better at night than during the day—partly due to customers "looking for the whorehouses. They wanted information and a place to park." He also said that Dorothy eventually left Vallejo and moved to Joe Conforte's Mustang Ranch brothel near Reno.

Gambling houses and bars continued to be a problem on Lower Georgia. The Aug. 18, 1943, *Vallejo Evening News Chronicle* carried a front-page story about a cashier at the Rex Club who was shot to death during an argument over poker chips. James Daniel, who had worked as a cabbie, was charged with the slaying of Bert McCloud. Daniel said he had no recollection of shooting McCloud, and his mind was blank until he "woke up" in the police station following the shooting. Daniel also said he had been drinking and had overdosed on a drug he had been taking to help him quit drinking alcohol. A jury later found Daniel guilty of first-degree murder, but he won an appeal that eased the judgment to second-degree murder. His sentence was a minimum five years in prison. Earlier in the year, auto court owner Antonio Garcia was accused of trying to kill cabbie Clarence Kessing at the Shipbuilders' Café, 222 Georgia St., where he had been playing cards. Police said Garcia began heckling Kessing after quitting the card game, and then pulled a knife and stabbed Kessing in the stomach. The Feb. 9, 1943, *Vallejo Evening Chronicle* reported that Garcia fled to Petaluma following the stabbing, and then went to Sacramento where, after conferring with his lawyer, he surrendered to police.

Another barroom slaying occurred at Lucky's Place, 519 Santa Clara St., on Sept. 24, 1942. In that case, Romeo d'Aloisio, one of the "Boys from Boston" in a Massachusetts-based Army unit assigned to guard Vallejo during the war, shot Annette Tipton several times after they quarreled and she ran away from him and into the tavern. The shot that hit her in the heart was listed as the cause of death. Arresting officers said the Army private admitted to shooting Tipton and stated, "She was no good. She was just a tramp and took me for everything I had." District Attorney Phillip Lynch demanded the death penalty, while d'Aloisio pleaded not guilty by reason of insanity. His lawyer said he was so drunk that he didn't realize what he was doing. The *Vallejo Evening Chronicle* reported on Feb. 9, 1943, that the soldier's trial ended with a "not guilty" verdict. In *The Boys from*

Boston, author Gary Cullen said, "The country was at war and patriotism was running high. Most of the witnesses were in Army green uniforms. The jury saw a poor soldier away from home, who, while trying to defend their community, was misled by a woman who intentionally used him for her own personal gain."

The North Star café and bar, at 146 Georgia St., was the scene of a Jan. 16, 1944, shooting spree by a former shipyard worker and Navy sailor who had been discharged from the military as a mental case. Bartender Marino Ranacis was killed and two others were wounded by Warren Astley, who "could give no coherent reason for his action. He babbled about 'faces before my eyes' and 'voices grating in my ears,'" the *Vallejo Times-Herald* reported the next day. The newspaper said Astley walked into the North Star, pulled out a revolver, shouted "Goodbye!" and began firing indiscriminately. Patrons, bartenders and waitresses scattered, running out doors and hiding behind and under tables. Astley had served aboard a ship in the South Pacific, and had been brought back from Guadalcanal as a mental case in mid-1943. He had been under treatment at a Navy hospital in Santa Cruz and had been discharged two weeks before the shootings. On April 6, 1944, Astley was declared insane following a Solano County Superior Court sanity hearing and was committed to a state mental hospital in Ukiah. A review of old court records showed no change in his custody status in later years.

While police were busy dealing with crime and trying to curtail prostitution, sailors, Marines and soldiers hanging out in bars in the Lower Georgia district could still drink on the cheap, thanks to action by the Vallejo War Price and Rationing Board. A front-page story in the March 2, 1944, *Vallejo Times-Herald* reported that more than three dozen taverns and bar operators agreed under pressure from the board to stop overcharging their patrons. "In most cases this will mean the ordinary drink, straight or in highballs, will be 35 cents instead of the average 40 to 50 cents, and in some instances even 60 cents, now charged," the newspaper said. "Western beer will be 15 cents and eastern beers up to 25 cents." The news account also stated the highest prices had been charged in the first block of Georgia Street, "where the bars are patronized almost exclusively by servicemen." The farther the bar patrons got from the waterfront, the lower the price of a drink would be—but the newspaper said the servicemen wouldn't bother to go bargain-hunting for a drink if it meant taking a bus or taxi.

CRITICS DEMAND MORE ENFORCEMENT EFFORTS

Despite the enforcement efforts in Vallejo, the round-the-clock action in the Lower Georgia district continued. That prompted the "Vigilante Committee of 500" to step up its efforts in mid-1944, with a demand that the city shut down known houses of prostitution and gambling. In a June 21, 1944, story, the *Vallejo Times-Herald* said the committee, inactive for more than a year, stated it was "aroused by the alarming increase in vice that threatens to throttle the healthy growth of Vallejo."

A resolution, read aloud at a committee meeting by the Rev. Lester Eisel of the First Presbyterian Church, named places noted in police court records as addresses "harboring gamblers and prostitutes." The resolution, quoted at length in the *Times-Herald,* stated that it was "an acknowledged fact that illegal gambling continues to flourish in Vallejo and vicinity in spite of the several raids by the police within the past few months at such places as 200 Capitol, 407 Santa Clara, the Pastime Club, Jay Bozeman's, 326 Virginia, 132 Georgia, 216½ Georgia, 112 Virginia, 317 Georgia, 130 Georgia, 108½ Georgia, 110 Georgia, 210 Virginia and 215 Georgia," and "equipment in these gambling places such as dice, dice cups, cards, chips, beans, dominoes, tables, chairs, race track paraphernalia, has not been regularly confiscated." The resolution also said prostitution "continues to exist in disregard to good public morals," adding that "prostitution arrests have been made at 239 Georgia, 213 Georgia and 141 Capitol" and "other well-known establishments are suspected of operating questionable practices." All the locations were in or near the Lower Georgia district.

The committee urged authorities to "diligently search out all places of gambling and prostitution, and confiscate every movable piece of gambling equipment," padlock all brothels and impose fines and jail time. The group also encouraged citizens to help "in ridding our city of all crime and corruption in high and low places by reporting all known violations of the law to the Citizens Committee."

Police Chief Dierking denied that vice in Vallejo was out of control, issuing a press release that stated, "Our record speaks for itself. Any time we see any violation of the law we will make arrests if the evidence warrants. We are enforcing the law to the best of our ability." But a citizens' committee member, shipyard employee Walter Robertson, stated at a July 17, 1944, City Council meeting that "either the police department does not know that gambling exists and refuses to be informed, or else the police department does know that gambling is flourishing in Vallejo and refuses to take corrective action." He also said the committee was creating a "war chest" to pay for its own investigators and lawyers in efforts to clean up the gambling and vice conditions.

Andrew Sheveland, the city's commissioner of health and safety, dismissed the claims made by the citizens' committee, saying Robertson's statement at the City Council meeting "cannot be considered a justifiable complaint. The police department of the city of Vallejo is ready and willing to act at all times in the best interests of the city, but we all recognize the fact that law enforcement agencies are limited to specific duties and activities, all of which must necessarily be based upon law and fact." Sheveland, quoted in a July 19, 1944, *Oakland Tribune* article, said, "It is not sufficient that rumors, inaccuracies and conjecture be acted upon to place in jeopardy citizens who, to the best of our knowledge, are law abiding. The organization calling itself a 'Committee of 500' has repeatedly made charges and circulated rumors but all efforts of the police department to pin them down to facts have so far failed."

Robertson told the City Council that he had gambled at one of the casinos to get evidence to support the citizens' group claims. That prompted Sheveland to say, "The police department cannot place itself in the position of compounding a felony to obtain evidence of law evasion even if the "Committee of 500' members feel that they can."

Gambling in the Lower Georgia district continued, prompting Navy Capt. G. C. Klein, the acting Mare Island commandant, to complain about an "unacceptable condition" causing problems for shipyard workers and sailors. Klein said he had been made aware of "the activities of professional gambling houses which are reported to be operating extensively in Vallejo." In a letter to the Vallejo City Council, printed in the Feb. 27, 1945, *Vallejo News Chronicle*, he added:

> Organized gambling in the City of Vallejo cannot be reconciled with the absolute necessity of keeping people on the job at their highest productive capacity at a time when all ships must be returned to combat in as short a time as possible. Cases of absenteeism, turnover, and debt delinquency which can be traced to the persevering efforts of the gamblers are evidence of this undesirable condition. Equally unsatisfactory is this situation as it affects military personnel, particularly those who go ashore for the first time in several months with large paychecks.

Faced with the Navy's insistence that gambling be suppressed and Mayor George C. Demmon's demand that "the law be enforced 100 percent," Sheveland stated in a Feb. 27, 1945, *Vallejo Evening News Chronicle* account that "conditions are gradually improving, and the law will be enforced. The chief of police has instructions to keep gambling at a minimum." That was followed by a March 6, 1945, *News Chronicle* story that the police department "announced that the lid is being clamped down on all gambling activities 'of any and all description' in this vicinity. This includes all illegal games of cards, dice, Chinese bean and button games, and even the lowly but profitable pastimes of bingo and punch boards." The newspaper added that with the move against bingo, "a storm of protest by lodges and other organizations followed, because of the fact that this form of entertainment had regularly been a Saturday night feature in various clubrooms." But Police Chief Dierking said, "The lid on gambling has been ordered clamped, and that means no exceptions."

Some of the clubs had been offering much more than bingo. Jack Flynn, longtime Vallejoan who ran the town's American Legion Hall during World War II, had a favorite story—one of many—about hiring one or two card dealers from Lower Georgia clubs to deal blackjack games at the hall on weekends. Slot machines also were in place. At one point, Flynn said he got a call from the police department warning him that the hall might be raided by state agents intent on stopping illegal gambling activity. He said he would need help getting the gambling equipment out of the hall, and a couple of the local cops showed up to give him a hand. After the state agents arrived, found no evidence of gambling and left, Flynn said he called the officers who had helped him clear out the gambling tables and slot machines. They returned to help him get the slots and tables back into the hall and ready for the weekend activities.

Vallejo native Ted Correy says the official line about gambling being under control doesn't match up with the stories he heard from his father, Tom "Tux" Correy, who had the Golden West Café, a bar at 241 Georgia St. Based on his father's accounts, gambling continued unabated in the Lower Georgia district during the war years.

"I overheard these stories at home when my dad and his friends were sitting around the dining table in the 1950s, gambling and laughing and telling stories about the war years, how they would make so much money that they wouldn't even count it," Correy said. "Many of the bars had basement gambling rooms, and they talked about tunnels that connected them. They had all sorts of stuff below Georgia Street. I heard there was a tunnel that went to the Bank of America (across the street from the Golden West Café, on the corner of Georgia and Sacramento streets), but I never saw it. That was the bank for the Lower Georgia Street bars. When the bars would close, they would put the money in a satchel and take it to a night deposit at the bank. The tellers would count it the next day, and the bar owners would come in and get a receipt. I think some insurance money went to the tellers, maybe a bonus, to keep them honest."

Correy says his uncle, George Rondis, also had a bar, George's Den, and told him his father was "a big-time gambler, one of the unofficial mayors of Lower Georgia Street. George told me that dad had ice-water in his veins, that he saw him bet $50,000 on one hand. He said that in a poker game dad would keep raising you until your nose would bleed. You can imagine how much money there was. The bars would stay open until 2 a.m. There were thousands of sailors. During the war, there would be standing room only. Sometimes you couldn't even get in a bar it was so crowded. During World War II, Lower Georgia Street was the No. 1 liberty call for sailors. If you could get to Lower Georgia, you were in heaven."

Among the many sailors who saw the Lower Georgia district during World War II were USS *Indianapolis* crewmembers, including Harold Bray, a 17-year-old from Northern Michigan who enlisted in the Navy in 1945 and following boot camp was sent to Mare Island to board the ship. "As far as Lower Georgia Street goes, I had a lot of liberties in Vallejo but I was too young to go into the bars. The older guys would go there," Bray said. "But I remember being on the deck of the ship, looking directly across the river down Georgia Street. All you could see were whitehats (sailors) and Marines. As far as you could see it was full of guys, a sea of whitehats bobbing along every day and every night. There wasn't any room for cars." After extensive repairs were completed, the big cruiser left Mare Island for Hunter's Point, where components of "Little Boy," the world's first operational atomic bomb, were loaded. The components were delivered to the island of Tinian on July 26, 1945. Four days later, headed to Leyte Gulf in the Philippines, the ship was torpedoed and sank. Of the 1,196 men aboard, about 900 made it into the water. After almost five days of shark attacks, starvation, thirst and exposure, 317 men including Bray were rescued.

On Aug. 6, 1945, an American B-29 bomber dropped "Little Boy" over Hiroshima. The explosion immediately killed 80,000 people. Three days later, a second B-29 dropped another A-bomb on Nagasaki, killing an estimated 40,000 people. Japan's Emperor Hirohito announced his country's unconditional surrender in an Aug. 15 radio address.

9

Lower Georgia Street Fades into History

On May 8, 1945, the Allies celebrated the defeat of Nazi Germany and the end of Adolf Hitler's Third Reich, formally recognizing the end of the Second World War in Europe. After six years and millions of lives lost, Hitler had committed suicide, German forces had surrendered unconditionally, and the war in Europe was finally over. That was followed by the United States' decision to drop two atomic bombs on Japan, resulting in the immediate deaths of 120,000 people and, several days later, the Aug. 15, 1945, announcement of Japan's surrender. Vallejoans' reaction to the announcement was described by the *Vallejo Times-Herald*:

> Screaming sirens and blasting horns heralded President Truman's declaration of peace, and throngs hysterical with joy paraded through the downtown streets.
>
> The news came just as thousands of Mare Island workers were changing shifts, and the homecoming war workers joined with the crowds of shoppers and servicemen who seemed to literally pour into the Georgia-Marin area. …
>
> Almost immediately after peace was announced, all local stores and bars closed their doors. A great number of eating-houses also shut their doors to celebrate the good news.
>
> A liquor shortage was not noticeable in the streets of Vallejo in spite of the tavern shutdown. VJ Day bottles were much in evidence and sailors and girls shared them in impromptu toasts along the sidewalks. Lipstick-smeared servicemen paraded the streets, singing at the top of their lungs and grabbing passing girls for victory kisses. Exploding firecrackers and improvised bombs added to the earsplitting din of sirens, horns, overturned garbage cans and general uproar.

Within four days after VJ Day, some 1,000 Mare Island Naval Shipyard employees quit work, "some without even collecting their pay checks," Arnold Lott wrote in *A Long Line of Ships*. The shipyard's contributions to the war effort included building and launching about 400 destroyers, submarines, landing craft, submarine tenders and other vessels. Hundreds of other ships underwent repairs. Prior to the war, Mare Island had a usable area of about 635 acres. That area had increased to about 1,500 acres by late 1945, when the shipyard returned to a five-day work week, the graveyard shift was ended and several thousand workers had been discharged. By mid-1946, the shipyard workforce had dropped by about 30,000 employees, back to pre-war levels. By 1947, the figure was down to about 10,000. But even though World War II was over, shipyard jobs were slashed and thousands of sailors, soldiers and Marines had left Mare Island and Vallejo, the Lower Georgia Street district was still alive—and still causing problems for authorities.

Efforts to stop prostitution in and around Vallejo continued, amid claims of possible ties between the bordellos and West Coast Mafia figures such as Jack Dragna, based in Southern California. A report from the U.S. Senate's Special Committee to Investigate Organized Crime in Interstate Commerce described Dragna as "one of the most notorious gangsters on the west coast. He is frequently referred to as the Capone of Los Angeles." The committee also said Dragna was "west coast representative for the Capone syndicate wire service" utilized by illegal bookmakers.

The claims of organized crime involvement in Vallejo prostitution gained some credence in January 1946 with an investigation into a chain of brothels operating in several California cities, including Vallejo, Stockton, Fresno, Oxnard and Bakersfield. The *Vallejo Times-Herald*, in a Jan. 22, 1946, report, described arrests of two men at a Newhall, California, mansion believed to have been the headquarters for the "white slavery" ring. Five alleged prostitutes also were arrested.

The *Times-Herald* said authorities believed the ring "ensnared hundreds of girls who were supplied to a chain of houses of prostitution. The chain-store system, it was said, furnished girls for Vallejo's bagnios, among many others." The two men, Lennie Gamble and Edward Clark, were arrested after one of their alleged victims, the daughter of a New Jersey industrialist, signed a complaint stating that Gamble beat her, breaking her jaw in four places. The complaint also alleged rape and assault with intent to do great bodily harm. Investigators said Hollywood waitresses and hat check girls were lured to the Newhall mansion on the pretense they were going to a party. Once there, they were given drugged drinks and marijuana and then were criminally attacked to "condition" them for prostitution. Police said operations of the ring were uncovered after the woman wrote a letter to a friend describing her plight. She gave the letter to a butler who, instead of mailing it, gave it to a Newhall justice of the peace who lived next door to the mansion.

More discussion of "big-time" crime in Vallejo developed in 1947, as Sheriff Thornton and Sam Vickers, Vallejo's first city manager, announced what they termed an all-out drive against vice and gambling. The year opened with Jan. 8 raids on five locations, all in or near the Lower Georgia district, where draw poker games were in progress. The raids occurred at the Rex, 215 Georgia St., the Laborers and Hodcarriers local at 210 Virginia St., the Labor Temple at 316 Virginia St., Bozeman's, 326 Virginia St., and Palace Billiards, 423½ Georgia St. "The raids were staged as part of the city council's campaign to rid Vallejo of gaming in any form," the *Vallejo News-Chronicle* reported. "While draw poker has been declared legal under state laws, it is prohibited under provisions of a city ordinance."

In an Oct. 17, 1947, *Oakland Tribune* article, both the sheriff's office and the police department announced formation of vice squads with order "to stamp out gambling, prostitution, dope peddling and other illegal activities," the newspaper reported. "Several big-time gamblers and vice operators have been endeavoring to move into Solano County and have found conditions not to their liking," Thornton said. Vickers said he had no evidence that professional gamblers had attempted to "invade Vallejo," the newspaper said. But the reform-minded city manager said prostitution, mainly in the Lower Georgia district, was a serious problem.

The anti-crime efforts coincided with a claim by state Attorney General Frederick Howser that Solano County was one of the state's prostitution "dark spots"—a statement that prompted Sheriff Thornton and Chief Dierking to say that Howser was off base. "Commercial houses (of prostitution) here are closed, have been closed and will remain that way," Dierking said in a letter to Howser. Sheriff Thornton added in a separate letter, reported by the Dec. 21, 1947, *Santa Cruz Sentinel*, that prostitution and vice conditions outside Vallejo's city limits were under control and he would welcome an investigation by the attorney general. The back-and-forth comments from Howser and the local officials were followed by a report from the state Department of Public Health that Solano County was one of 18 counties where "established prostitution" was flourishing. Finally, the Dec. 27, 1947, *Vallejo Times-Herald* quoted both Thornton and Dierking as saying there were no known houses of prostitution in the entire county. "Every chief of police in the county has submitted written reports to me that they know of no houses of prostitution in their respective cities," Thornton said. "I certainly resent the health department's charge that there are any." Dierking added, "There is no prostitution here. Everything is tight and has been for some time so far as we know." Dr. Alvin Leonard, acting county health officer, said that the state charge might have been warranted in the past, but he believed the prostitution problem had been remedied since creation of the Vallejo Police Department's vice squad, which was "moving in the right direction" with its investigations and arrests.

Several months later, the *Fresno Bee* reported on May 17, 1948, that Sheriff Thornton had led a gambling raid which was "the biggest operation of its kind in the history of Solano County." The raid by three carloads of deputies resulted in the arrests of 109 people at a chicken ranch on Benicia Road, several miles east of Vallejo. Thornton said the gambling operation featured chuck-a-luck, dominoes, a lottery and other games, and had been set up by the Far Eastern Company syndicate. The raid was followed by the shutdown of a bookmaking operation at McNamee Billiards, 237 Georgia St., reported June 3, 1948, by the *Vallejo Times-Herald*. The newspaper said three men were arrested at the location, described by District Attorney Phillip Lynch as "a room where there was paraphernalia for the purpose of recording and registering bets and wages on horse racing."

Two weeks later, in a surprise move, City Manager Vickers fired Dierking, telling the police chief the reason for his dismissal was "your failure to reasonably cooperate with this office." Vickers also announced that Police Lt. Jack Stiltz, who had been named by Dierking several months earlier to head the department's vice squad, would be taking over as police chief. The announcement, detailed in a June 17, 1948, *Vallejo Times-Herald* story, was made at a stormy city council meeting attended by about 150 people, many of them friends of Dierking. At the meeting, Dierking insisted that he had done a good job as chief and said he deserved a full explanation from Vickers—who repeated the charge of a lack of cooperation but offered no more details. "That's the only charge I've made," Vickers said, adding, "I'm not going to start throwing mud … my conscience is very clear on this."

With Stiltz in charge, efforts to shut down vice in Vallejo intensified—but brothels were still operating. Joe Conforte, who went on to create the well-known Mustang Ranch brothel near Reno, said that in the early 1950s he got the inspiration to get into the prostitution business while driving a cab and taking fares from Oakland to Vallejo's whorehouses. In his *Breaks, Brains and Balls*, co-authored by David Toll, Conforte said he gave a ride to a prostitute who told him to call if a fare was looking for "some action." A few days later he brought her a sailor, picked him up an hour later and got a $3 tip from the hooker, who charged the sailor $10. "Now I'm beginning to see that this was a good deal," Conforte said of his 30 percent cut in addition to the cab fare, adding, "Vallejo was open at that time, and now I'm hustling loads of soldiers and sailors to take them to Vallejo, 30 miles from Oakland. Not only did that make a good cab fare, but I also made 30 percent of what they spent. My commission was more than my paycheck. So I liked it." During the years he ran the Mustang Ranch, Conforte gave cabbies who brought him customers the same 30 percent cut.

Nick Razes recalls a "doorman" job he had as a boy during the summer at his father's Vallejo Grille, 204 Georgia St., letting a few sailors in once a few others had finished eating. It was just after World War II and Georgia Street was still crowded with people. "My dad also had the St. Francis Rooms above the Vallejo Grille," Razes said. "He charged the sailors by the hour for the rooms. There were lots of hookers working Lower Georgia Street. Sailors and girls were going up the stairs at all hours. He paid off his home in three years." Razes also said that he and his sister, who ran the cash register at the restaurant, were able to watch movies for free at the Valmar theater next door—but were told by their father to not go anywhere else in the district.

It was clear that Police Chief Stiltz was having an impact with his reform efforts. His son, Jack Stiltz Jr., said his father started getting death threats—and at one point even got a tip from an informant that two would-be assassins, armed with machine-guns, were outside his home.

"My mom and dad went to a New Year's Eve party at the Casa de Vallejo Hotel. It was 1949 or 1950," Stiltz said. "We had a babysitter for my sister and me. The phone rang, and it was my dad's snitch from Lower Georgia Street. He told the babysitter to get ahold of Jack Stiltz and tell him to come home in the alley, that there were two guys across the street from the house with machine guns and they were going to kill him. The next thing I remember was the street all lit up out in front. Dad had the house surrounded. They caught two guys who were laying in the lot across the street from the house. They were going to mow down my mom and dad. I just remember vividly seeing all the commotion that was going on. My mom was scared to death after that. She had blinds put in the front windows so she could keep them pulled down."

"Dad got the threats because police were closing up all the gambling joints and the prostitution," his son said. "I don't know for a fact whether some of the old cops had been taking payoffs before that." Stiltz also said his father told him how one of his officers "showed up on our front porch with a suitcase full of money from a circus that was in town. They wanted to have gambling. Dad told the cop to get his ass off the porch and take the money back."

Stiltz also recalled leaving with his family for a summer vacation in the mountains, but turning around after only a couple of hours on the road because he had an apparent appendicitis attack. "Dad had been able to shut down the gambling and prostitution on Georgia Street, but as soon as he left on vacation it opened back up," Stiltz said. "They knew he would be gone. It's a good thing he did come back early. Otherwise he might have lost his job."

The anti-vice efforts continued, including a May 29, 1949, raid resulting in the arrests of seven women working in two rooming house brothels and a male cabbie accused of soliciting for one of the locations, the Shasta Rooms at 220 Georgia St. The other location was the Empress Hotel, at 426 Santa Clara St. The cabbie was fined $300. A 30-day jail sentence imposed by Police Judge Wallace Cox was "suspended on the promise of good behavior," the *Vallejo Evening News Chronicle* reported. The women, most of them charged with living in and about a house of ill fame and quarantined by public health officials, were hit with fines ranging from $500 to $1,500.

On Jan. 4, 1950, the city Council revoked the business licenses of the Shasta Rooms and the Royal Rooms at 219½ Georgia St., and was advised of a license surrender at the Cozy Rooms, 239 Georgia St. Prostitution arrests had occurred at all three locations.

In another raid, reported in the Oct. 17, 1950, *Vallejo Times-Herald*, officers combed the lower downtown areas in a drive on vice and gambling but made no arrests. Chief Stiltz charged that "outside interests, possibly aided by some Vallejoans, had attempted to open the town to gambling and vice." Stiltz added that he was convinced "there were attempts being made to create a 'little Reno' in the lower downtown area of Vallejo," the newspaper said. When officers showed up, "the suspected 'joints' closed up or went underground,"

Stiltz said, adding that the patrols in the area would continue and his officers were ordered to "hit and hit hard whenever there is evidence of gambling or vice."

Tip-offs to "suspected joints" were a problem for Stiltz. Jay Bozeman, a nationally known billiards player, had a billiards hall at 326 Virginia Street—and he also had gambling and a bookmaking operation. His daughter, Sharon Bozeman Nunn, says the story she heard from her mother was "that someone high up in City Hall would call dad when any investigators were going to come in. He would shut down the gambling and bookmaking, and he wouldn't reopen until he got another call that it was OK to reopen."

The police chief's job had its lighter moments, including the time his sister, Jean Raahauge, got him to return a set of false teeth to the Cavern, a basement-level dive bar at 222B Georgia St. Marjorie Riley, my mother, wrote about it in a humorous *Vallejo Independent Press* newspaper column, entitled "*Uncle Jake's False Teeth.*" Jean's elderly uncle Jake returned from a local bar one evening minus his teeth. Nobody at that bar had seen any teeth, but Jean spotted an ad from the Cavern stating that some false teeth had been found there. Jake refused to go to the bar, so Jean convinced Marjorie, her good friend, to go with her. They tried to retrieve the teeth quietly, but the bar owner made a big show of things and everyone was listening in. Finally, Marjorie and Jean fled with the teeth and rushed over to Jake's house. He popped the teeth in his mouth—but they didn't fit. Jean couldn't believe it, and tried to help by pushing the teeth back into his mouth. "Uncle Jake began to gag. The teeth protruded rather like a beaver's teeth," Marjorie wrote. "We tried not to laugh, but it was too much." Uncle Jake was not amused, and said the teeth should go back to the bar. Jean lacked the nerve to do that, so she turned to her brother. "The chief did it, but reluctantly," Marjorie wrote. "He looked like he might have preferred chasing a bank robber down Georgia Street."

Police found themselves doing some unexpected marriage counseling in what they termed "the unique story of 1949," the *Oakland Tribune* reported on Jan. 21, 1949. Officers said a man having a drink at the Navy Café, 207 Georgia St., started discussing marriage with a barmaid and he agreed to marry her. "The bartender spoke up and said he would perform the ceremony," Will Baker told police. "He asked us several questions, pronounced us man and wife, and charged me $3. My bride took a piece of paper from the bartender, which he said was the license, and left. I haven't seen her since. And what I want to know is this: am I legally married?"

The Kefauver Committee Sheds Light on the Mob

While prostitution and gambling were still part of the Lower Georgia scene in the post-war years, local reform efforts were helped greatly by hearings held by the U.S. Senate into illegal gambling and mob activity around the country. On May 3, 1950, the Senate established a five-member Special Committee to Investigate Organized Crime in Interstate Commerce. Estes Kefauver, an ambitious freshman senator from Tennessee, was named committee chairman. The panel visited fourteen major cities in fifteen months, grilling mobsters and amassing reams of material on gangland activities.

The Kefauver Committee's report included details about race wires utilized by bookmakers—and tolerated or ignored by authorities in many cases. Several Vallejo locations and individuals in or within a block or two of the Lower Georgia district were listed as clients of Pioneer News Service, a major race wire. The California Public Utilities Commission also held lengthy hearings into the wire network that fed track results to subscribers all over the state, including the service feeds, or "drops," in Vallejo. An *Associated Press* story that ran on the front page of the Feb. 26, 1948, *Vallejo Times-Herald* listed drops to Jay Bozeman at 326 Virginia St. and at 423½ Georgia St., Willy Musso at the Rex Club, 215 Georgia St., the Mint Smoke Shop and A.C. McNamee's billiards hall, both listed at 237 Georgia St., Harrison Reade at 317 Virginia St., and John Farrell at the Sports Club liquor store, 216 Georgia St. All the drops had been operating since late May 1946. Three were disconnected in 1947 and four others were disconnected in early 1948 as investigations into racing wires began and new state penalties for bookmaking took effect.

During questioning at the PUC hearings by Warren Olney, attorney for Gov. Earl Warren's commission on organized crime, Western Union executive J. B. Norcross said the race information was transmitted to Vallejo by *Pioneer News Service*, which leased its wire from Western Union. The PUC also learned that information from eastern tracks was flashed into California by way of a wire loop connecting Chicago with California outlets—and that virtually nothing had been done by law enforcement agencies to stop the race wire service from going to known bookmakers. The wire services, barred from racetracks, typically hired "wigwaggers," people at the tracks who used a system of hand signals to relay information such as up-to-the-minute horse or jockey changes, weather and track conditions—details that bookies needed to ensure a successful betting operation. The "wigwaggers" would be monitored by confederates using binoculars or telescopes. Then the latest information would be relayed by phone to the wire services. Getting the wire, according to the Kefauver Committee's report, was "as essential to a bookmaker as a stock ticker to a stock broker."

In a move described by Olney as a death blow to a large-scale bookmaking racket, authorities struck at the leased wires used by *Pioneers News Service*, asking Western Union and Pacific Telephone & Telegraph Co. to discontinue their facilities at Pioneer's penthouse headquarters in San Francisco's business district. Both utilities acted promptly to comply, Morrie Landsberg of the *Associated Press* reported on Feb. 27, 1948. The California Legislature followed up with two new laws aimed at driving slot machines out of the state. Gov. Earl Warren said in signing the new laws on April 26, 1950, that they and the PUC action against the race wires were "perhaps the two things which can be made to do the most to cut off the profits of the underworld." Congress then approved a law, signed Jan.

2, 1951, by President Truman, prohibiting transportation of gambling devices across state lines. The law also banned slot machines on land under federal jurisdiction. Mare Island and other military bases immediately removed and destroyed the "one-armed bandits" that had been in clubs for officers and non-coms.

Gambling action on Lower Georgia had been a big deal through the World War II boom years and for a few years afterwards, but those days were winding down as scrutiny from authorities increased. Nevada, where wide-open gambling was legal, was a drive of only a few hours to the east, and some of Vallejo's best-known Lower Georgia club operators headed to the neighboring Silver State. They included Curly Musso of the Rex Club, 215 Georgia St., Norman Reinburg of Dopey Norman's at 124 Georgia St., and George Canon of the C & S Sportland and Locker Club, at 210 Georgia St. Their first stop in Nevada was the tiny community of Stateline, on Lake Tahoe's south shore. Curly Musso and George Canon opened the Gateway Club in May 1949 in a Quonset hut just across the Nevada line. Next door, Reinburg briefly ran another Dopey Norman's club. After selling their property to Bill Harrah in 1955, for his first gaming venture at Tahoe, Musso and Canon joined in pioneering Heavenly Valley Ski Resort. Musso also served in various executive posts at Harrah's Tahoe until retiring in 1974.

While some of the "smart money" club operators were leaving town, a mid-1950s city directory still showed twenty licensed bars, sixteen restaurants, seventeen boarding houses and hotels and a couple of liquor stores in the Lower Georgia district. It may have been getting seedier, but remained a favorite hangout for sailors on liberty from their ships tied up at Mare Island. The good times continued, and pressure for demolition of the Lower Georgia district increased.

The September 1952 edition of *Eye*, one of New York publishing entrepreneur Martin Goodman's many magazines, led off with an expose entitled "Vice Booms in Vallejo." The story claimed that Vallejo's Lower Georgia district had 40 brothels "at its sinful peak," located mainly in rooming houses and second-floor hotels above bars. The article also described repeated efforts in the early 1950s by City Manager Al Wanger to shut down the brothels, and how that led to a move by some bordello operators from the Lower Georgia district to locations outside the Vallejo city limits. For several years, one of those locations was in the Glen Cove area, just off the highway leading from Vallejo to nearby Benicia. The article also said one enterprising Vallejo madam named Ginger even turned a houseboat into a floating whorehouse that made a few trips upriver to a Suisun Bay location to attract airmen and workers at Travis Air Force Base. According to a Feb. 26, 1952, *UPI* report, Vallejoans Willy Musso and Lee Bassett set up a bookmaking operation on an old riverboat in Benicia. The news story said Bassett, testifying at a state hearing, told how he and Musso turned the boat "into a social club and admitted point-blank the establishment was primarily used for bookie operations." The riverboat bookmaking shut down in April 1951, Bassett added.

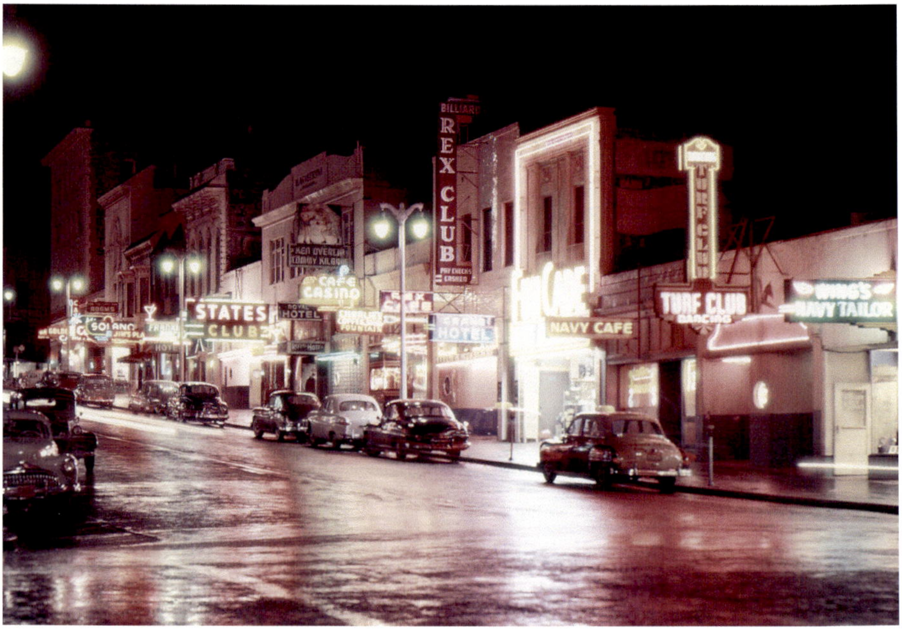

Following a light nighttime rain in the early 1950s, Thomas W. Atkinson Jr. took this time-lapse photo of the 200 block of Lower Georgia Street. *[Thomas W. Atkinson Jr. photo]*

Interest in urban renewal was increasing throughout the nation in the 1950s, and Vallejo was no exception—especially since the Lower Georgia district was still a source of all sorts of problems even though the boom World War II years were over. Those problems included a gang fight that left one man, Richard Zirkel, dead. A Sept. 1, 1954, *Vallejo Times-Herald* article said the fight involved about 20 men, half sailors and the other half civilians. Police Lt. James Booras said Zirkel suffered from a rheumatic heart and that may have caused his death rather than any blows struck. The officer also said one witness stated there had been "an exchange of words" between the groups and that Zirkel had tried "to stop any fisticuffs by telling the sailors to 'lay off,' or words to that effect." Instead, Zirkel was knocked down by a sailor and kicked. He was pronounced dead on arrival at a local hospital.

One of the last big Lower Georgia problems occurred in 1956, when thousands of motorcyclists and spectators showed up in Vallejo for a weekend racing event. Along with the races, there were brawls, injuries and property damage to some Lower Georgia bars. The *Vallejo Times-Herald*, in a May 27, 1956, front-page story, compared the violence to the 1947 rioting by thousands of bikers in Hollister, California, that inspired the 1953 film *The Wild One*, starring Marlon Brando. Police Chief Stiltz called in extra peace officers from several agencies, and officers made at least a dozen arrests and issued more than 80 citations for drunkenness, fighting, disturbing the peace, speeding and muffler violations. About

2,000 motorcyclists signed up for the American Motorcycle Association's annual Northern California Gypsy Tour and Rally, and many "outlaw" bikers and spectators also were on hand. One motorcyclist who signed up for the organized event, which featured races at a speedway on the edge of town, groused about "the booze fighters and the hot-rodders," adding, "The only reason that outlaw bunch shows up at these things is to raise hell and try to disrupt things." The result, the *Times-Herald* reported, was "the most excitement Vallejo has seen since V-J Day" as "wild 'outlaw' cyclists turned the lower end of Georgia street into one big drag strip for races, and thousands of curious Vallejoans jammed the sidewalks to watch." The paper added that harassed police decided to "block off the 200 block of Georgia street and 'let 'em go to it' last night in an effort to keep under control both the roving drivers and the thousands of Vallejoans who thronged the downtown area to see the excitement." Finally, as "fast and furious" racing continued late into the night, police managed to stop the races by calling for a fire truck to wet down the street. By the end of the weekend, one biker was hospitalized in critical condition with a fractured skull and dozens of others were nursing bruises, abrasions, cuts and lacerations. Rowdy barroom patrons trashed some Lower Georgia businesses, including one bar where "the floor was virtually an inch deep in broken glasses and beer bottles plus a generous amount of assorted filth and debris," the *Times-Herald* said. "This isn't the only place. We can show you quite a few others," an officer told reporters. As an eleven-year-old paperboy, I read that story in the morning paper and took a detour of a few blocks from my usual route to see the damage for myself. Broken glass spread out through one bar's front doors, hanging wide open at 6 a.m., carpeting the sidewalk. The place looked like it had been destroyed.

The Lure of the Lower Georgia District

The Lower Georgia district's reputation was known far and wide. In his *Yeah, What Else?* collection of essays and poems, Vallejo native Charlie Spooner recounted a conversation with a cousin, a 30-year Navy veteran: "He assured me that Lower Georgia was notorious throughout the Pacific Fleet. Every sailor knows of our town and its special enterprise zone. If memory serves, his exact words were, 'You could buy or sell anything there, Charlie.' It took a while for the many implications of that statement to sink in. Which brings us back to the original question: was Lower Georgia that dangerous, notorious place your parents warned you about? Or was it simply a colorful neighborhood, anchored by enduring institutions and possessing a certain faded beauty? I prefer the colorful neighborhood version. Though I have to admit, if I was raising my kids in Vallejo during the forties and fifties, they would hear from me in no uncertain terms: Don't you ever let me catch you down there." Spooner also tells a funny story about his mother who, after hearing his father talk about the Lower Georgia joints, suggested that they go dancing some evening. The

Spooners' dance date at a Lower Georgia club ended abruptly when one patron, a woman wearing a coat, shifted on her bar stool. The coat opened slightly—and Mrs. Spooner realized the woman was a prostitute and the coat was all she was wearing.

Maureen Sheehan Moore, who had orders from her parents to stay away from Lower Georgia, says, "There was one rule: you just didn't step off the curb at Sacramento Street and go any further down Georgia Street. You couldn't. I wasn't supposed to go there because of all the honky-tonks and prostitution that was going on. We could go down there every Friday with mom to get fish at Parmisano's fish market. When mom would say she was going, we couldn't wait. We would go so that we could listen to everything. Lower Georgia Street was full of sailors, music, honky-tonks. It was glorious to a young girl who wasn't used to that kind of thing."

One evening, Maureen was playing with friends outside her home several blocks from Lower Georgia, and one of the boys talked her into breaking the no-Lower Georgia rule: "A few of us went into the alley behind the Rex Rooms (boarding house) and climbed up some old wooden steps. I looked in a window, and it was the first time I ever saw a naked man. He had been visiting one of the girls, and was putting his clothes back on. At the time, this was a big deal. Plus, we didn't usually disobey my mother. I didn't tell her about that for years and years."

On another Lower Georgia expedition in the early 1950s, Maureen went to Love's record store to buy a record. She was so nervous about disobeying her parents that she blurted out the name of the record—"I Want To Be Your Baby"—but said nothing else. The surprised store owner and a couple of others in the small shop all started laughing, and an embarrassed Maureen ran out of the store, minus the record. Jodean Spinelli Coakley, who also had been told by her parents to avoid the Lower Georgia Street district, went to the same store to buy a copy of "Annie Had a Baby." She made the purchase, but felt so bad about disobeying her parents that she confessed to the "sin" in her next visit to St. Vincent Ferrer Catholic Church, a few blocks away. My sister Ellen Riley McClure and her friends would challenge similar parental edicts by waiting on the "good" side of Georgia Street, the 300 block, at the intersection of Sacramento Street, until the traffic signal turned green. Then they would run across the street, tap a toe on the "bad" side, the 200 block of Georgia Street, and run back before the light turned red. Carolyn Hewitt Brown, daughter of G. Wilfred Hewitt who served as Vallejo mayor from 1955 to 1963, told an identical story. Former City Council member Joanne Morriss Schivley, a Vallejo native, says she would occasionally walk up Georgia Street with her mother, who would return by ferry from her shipyard job to the Vallejo side of the river and then walk up Georgia Street to stores in the 300 block, just beyond the bar zone. "I was told to not get too close to the bars, or they would grab you and drag you inside," Schivley said. "I can remember walking as close to the curb as possible."

While warnings to avoid Lower Georgia Street were the norm, some young Vallejoans seemed to come and go as they pleased—especially if they were delivering newspapers.

Francisco Lopez, ten years old when he started delivering the *San Francisco Call-Bulletin* in the district in the mid-1950s, described his paper route as "my ticket to getting a free education." Lopez recalls seeing sailors fighting in the streets, drunks in pool halls and prostitutes plying their trade in flea-bag boarding houses. "I was intrigued by all of this," Lopez said. "If I had any common sense I probably should have been scared. But I was young and naïve. I may have got myself into some dangerous situations, but I never was robbed or pushed around. It was an adventure."

Lopez also nosed around some of the colorful businesses such as Doc Webb's tattoo parlor, a fixture at 230A Georgia St. for years until Doc Webb relocated to San Diego's old Gas Lamp district. I did the same, as did classmate Dann Shively. "I'd love to watch him tattoo sailors and carve totem poles," Shively said. "I would check out the drawings of scantily clad women on his walls. They were samples of what you could have tattooed. My main interests there were the magic tricks and 'novelties.' What 11-year-old could pass up fake dog crap or a joy buzzer?" Other "novelties": A nickel glued to the floor, plastic barf, whoopee cushions, skull rings, exploding cigarettes and a small box labeled "Oddities of the World." Inside the box was a statue of a beautiful woman with her breasts bared—all three of them.

Shively and Vallejo native Billy Gordon also shared stories about a Lower Georgia district pharmacy that hired teenagers to make deliveries. Gordon said a shipyard co-worker, Jack Kopf, would talk about delivering medical prescriptions to prostitutes working in whorehouses in the district in the 1930s. Shively said that as a college student in the 1960s he worked part-time at another pharmacy with Ed Grigg, who had owned the Lower Georgia drug store. Grigg would tell a similar story about one of the delivery boys, Raymond Burr. Shively said that during his long news career at KCRA-TV, Sacramento, he was able to ask Burr about Grigg's tale. Burr, being interviewed at the station in the early 1990s for an upcoming *Perry Mason* movie, confirmed the story. "We had a good laugh over the fact that I thought Eddy was just telling tall tales about a big star," Shively said. "I finally learned the truth, after 25 years."

The Lower Georgia district continued its downhill slide in the late 1950s. Frank Darling recalls helping his father, Gordon Darling, at his furniture store and at his Charlotte Hotel on Sacramento Street, and seeing "all the winos and bums who were around there. I was just a kid and I would rub elbows with them." Darling also recalled being routinely sent to a nearby cigar store to get change for his father, with the clerk at the cigar store "giving me a non-verbal 'be careful' look if there was someone around who looked like trouble. Seeing all those things conditioned me. You know how the other side lives. You're a little less horrified about things like Lower Georgia Street." Darling also talked about some of the efforts by his father's aunt, Police Matron Rose Milestein, to help women in the district, including prostitutes who had been roughed up by pimps. Milestein, hired in 1944 as the city's first police matron, also was very active in the Salvation Army. "She was tough-looking and tough-acting," Darling said. "She would come across as a very cold person, but she was very helpful and would do anything for anybody. If a girl got beat up, she would help them. Sometimes she would call dad if someone needed a ride. He had a car and she didn't drive. He just did what she told him to do. He was an orphan and she was an anchor for him—a surrogate mother."

END OF THE LINE DRAWS CLOSE FOR VALLEJO'S BARBARY COAST

In a May 26, 1957, column, *Vallejo Times-Herald* Managing Editor Wyman Riley, my father, said the time had finally arrived for demolition of the now-blighted Lower Georgia district.

The district was "once the match for any sailorman's dream street from Brooklyn to Singapore, sought after for its flesh-pots and feared for its violence," Riley wrote in support of the redevelopment project that eventually bulldozed the entire district. He added:

> Lower Georgia street today is a tawdry, tired, worn-out old harridan, trying to live down her past and wearing, unsteadily, a slightly tarnished and unfamiliar crown of respectability, not quite sure about what happened when the lights went out some 10 or 12 years ago but well aware that the glittering tinsel is gone. The playboys, the playgirls, the gamblers, the shills, the tough guys and the "hot" guys, the thrill-seekers and the "tourists," they've all left her without so much as a second thought.
>
> But if there are any second thoughts, they'd be lively ones. There are many who remember the brightly lighted street—and its not-so-brightly-lighted alleys—with mingled feelings, perhaps even shock. Or apprehension. Or misgiving. Generally the stories they tell of the lower blocks are prefaced with: "I was never in one of the places myself, but a fellow told me ... "
>
> The street had its good guys and bad guys, the brave ones and the cowards, the skinflints and the open-hearted. It was a patchwork quilt of the best and the worst of humanity, and the comings and goings of its motley throngs made more gossip than news, much of it spread by word-of-mouth to the far corners of the earth.
>
> In the lower blocks, there flourished saloons, dance halls and various sin palaces. Before the turn of the century (1900) there was outrage at the way in which sailors were treated, beaten up, robbed and sometimes murdered. Sandbagging and an early-day version of mugging were familiar reports to a scant police force. There were fights and riots and those without business there avoided the place. This was not an unusual situation; it was part of waterfront life in a seaport town.

Riley wrote that the district was Vallejo's first business area, the heart of the city with many "name" firms. But as Vallejo expanded, most "name" businesses moved away from the waterfront and the lower blocks began catering to businesses that were mostly "illegal and frowned upon." His column concluded:

> By the time World War II and its 24-hour day arrived, lower Georgia street was a going concern. There was more neon in the 200 block than in any other single city block in the world. And as crowded as the street was with shipyard and military personnel seeking respite from the tensions of job and war, the alleys were almost as well-patronized.
>
> There was packed into a two-block square area more action than any other place in California. Wine (in the form of bad booze in equally bad bars), Women (uncounted hundreds of them), and Song (from blaring juke boxes piped out onto the street), Chinese lotteries behind laundry fronts, gambling behind steel doors, and dice games at cigar counters—they were all part of the pattern.
>
> But the old street didn't realize there was a limit to how high she could live it up and she died from an overdose of illicit gaiety. She became too brazen and suddenly the roof fell in. Most of the street's purveyors of entertainment took it on the Arthur Duffy out of town. Others unwilling or unable to believe that the end was at hand tried to stick it out. To many, it was fatal, uncomfortable and unprofitable. Eventually they all left.
>
> Just as the lower blocks once had better days, so, we think, they will again—when urban redevelopment moves in to create a new Lower Georgia Street and begin another era in its long and colorful history.

Redevelopment had many advocates—among them Luther Gibson, publisher of the morning *Vallejo Times-Herald* and afternoon *Vallejo News-Chronicle*. Gibson's power base and political connections extended from Sacramento, where he served as a leading Democratic state senator, to Washington, D.C., the source of federal redevelopment dollars. But redevelopment also had its critics. They included attorney Jack Burstein, who started practicing law in Vallejo in the mid-1950s, in an office on Georgia Street, a half block from the Lower Georgia district. Burstein says his first impression of the Lower Georgia district was "a place that was buzzing all the time. What a pity to tear it down. That was the worst tragedy that ever happened to Vallejo, in my opinion, because you had thriving traffic going back and forth, and it became dead because of so-called redevelopment. We're still waiting for redevelopment to happen. How long has it been? Fifty or sixty years and it still hasn't happened. Without redevelopment, Vallejo would still have a thriving downtown."

Burstein was well aware of what the district had been during World War II: "With the outbreak of the war, the city just became a boomtown. People who had had no money for the previous eight or ten years because of the Great Depression suddenly were making money and wanted to spend it. For the first time in ten years they were able to live. And on Lower Georgia you would have a bar at the street level, gambling in the basement and a whorehouse upstairs. A lot of them were just exactly that. When I came to Vallejo, prostitution had pretty much stopped. My law partner had represented most of the madams, and some of them were still coming in. I rented a room in a boarding house that not too long before had been a whorehouse."

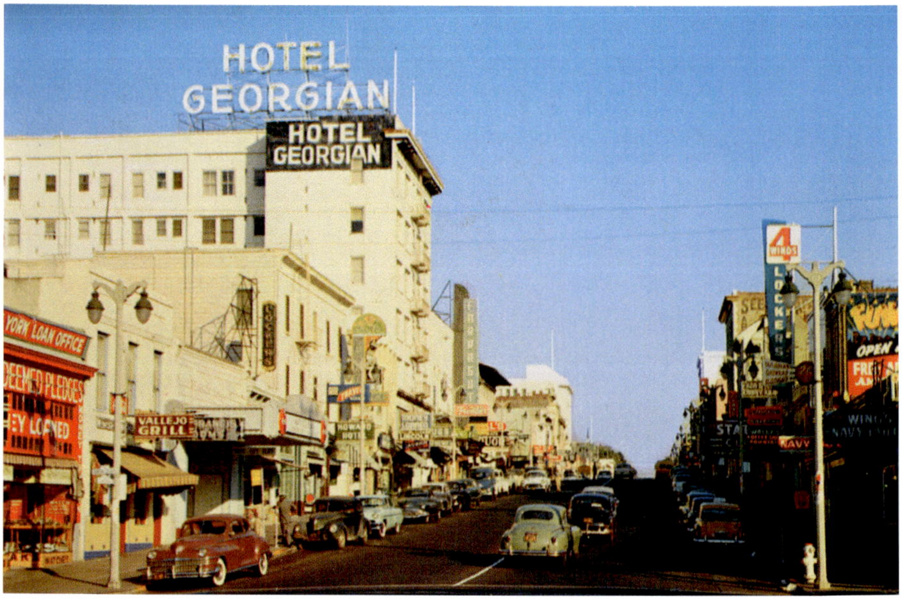

This World War II-era photo was taken at the intersection of Georgia and Santa Clara streets, looking eastward into the 200 block of Georgia Street, the heart of the sailors' territory. *[Vallejo Naval and Historical Museum]*

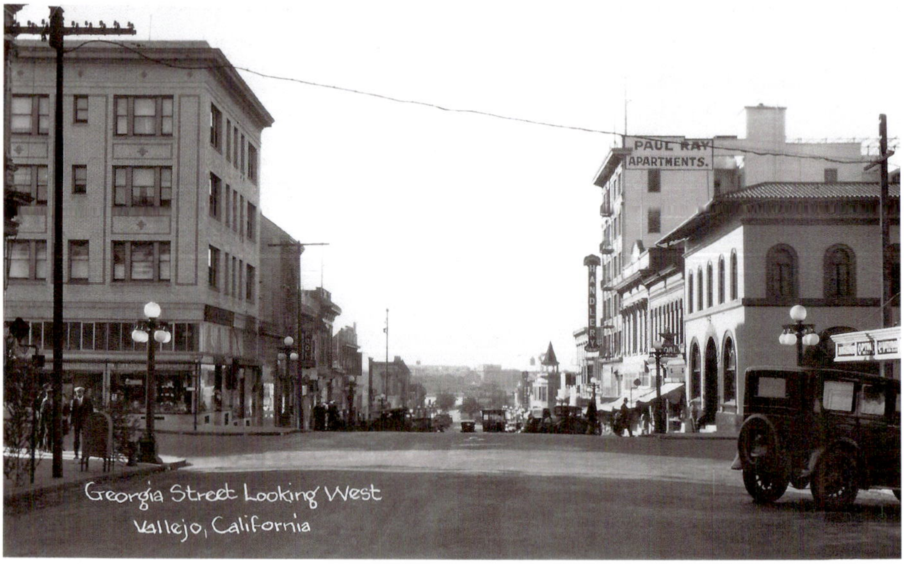

This photo was taken near the intersection of Georgia and Sacramento streets, looking west from the "respectable" 300 block of Georgia Street into the 200 block, in the infamous "Barbary Coast" zone. *[Vallejo Naval and Historical Museum]*

Longtime Vallejo resident and businessman Mike Coakley questions whether the Lower Georgia District that he saw, while working for the phone company in the late 1950s, ever could have been revived. "You just didn't go to the bars down there at night," Coakley said. "If you did, it was because you were looking for trouble. That's the way it was until redevelopment." Coakley added that he was working on the telephone service at a rooming house on the edge of the Lower Georgia district in 1957 and, seeing men and women going in and out of rooms, realized he was in a brothel. Suddenly, an earthquake hit, the building began to shake and people began screaming. It turned out to be a minor quake, but for a moment Coakley said he thought, "If I don't make it out of this place alive, God is not going to believe why I was here."

Bulldozers and Wrecking Balls

Redevelopment began in earnest under Mayor Wilfred Hewitt, elected in 1955, and continued under his successor, Florence Douglas, mayor from 1963 to 1979. By 1970, several hundred structures on about 24 blocks of Vallejo's original downtown and adjacent side streets were leveled. Under the massive, federally funded urban renewal program, even the York Street hill on which the Capitol of California once stood was bulldozed flat. The earth was hauled a short distance to the riverfront and used to extend Vallejo's shoreline. Among the demolished structures was the Navy YMCA building, built in hopes of giving sailors a better option than the dive bars and boarding houses in the Lower Georgia district; the landmark Astor House, originally the Metropolitan House, built in 1859 before Abraham Lincoln became president; the Vallejo Women's Club, originally designed as a YWCA by famed architect Julia Morgan; the eight-story Georgian Hotel; a Bank of America branch; and the city's beautiful Andrew Carnegie Library—the final and most controversial target of redevelopment, torn down in 1970.

My brother, Michael Riley, recalls how he and some teenage friends got into the old Bank of America building at 240 Georgia St., just before it was torn down, by pulling some boards off a window and climbing in. "Two of us found the bank vault. A key on a ring with several other keys was in the huge vault door. The vault door was open, so we went inside. There were boxes and boxes of blank, uncanceled checks and other papers," he said. "But we decided against a life of crime. We didn't rob the bank. We left all that stuff inside the vault."

When the Naval Base Cafe building at 147 Georgia St. was demolished in July 1962, as part of the redevelopment project, workers made a grim discovery: a dungeon-like basement that was secure as any prison, with thick brick walls, barred windows and individual cells sealed off by massive doors. The structure was built in 1870 on the southwest corner of Georgia and Santa Clara streets by early-day Vallejo businessman Philip Bernard Lynch.

Lynch, a native of Ireland who came to Vallejo in 1858, ran a grocery store on the main floor and lived with his family on the second floor.

When the building was torn down, Lynch's grandson, then-Superior Court Judge Philip Lynch, recalled that the basement was used as a storeroom for the grocery store. He wasn't certain that it was used as a jail but agreed that it could have been after the Lynch family sold the property, prior to the war years. Vallejo native and Superior Court Judge Paul Beeman had an answer to the puzzle, recounting a story he heard many times from his father: During World War II, military police used the dungeon as a temporary brig for sailors and Marines who had been picked up for causing trouble in bars or on the street. Beeman said the lockup was created by breaking through the basement walls of the Lynch Building into an old, brick-lined sewer system that hadn't been used for years. Locked gates and bars were installed, and straw was tossed on the floor. There were no toilets and no water. "It was almost as bad as water-boarding," Beeman said.

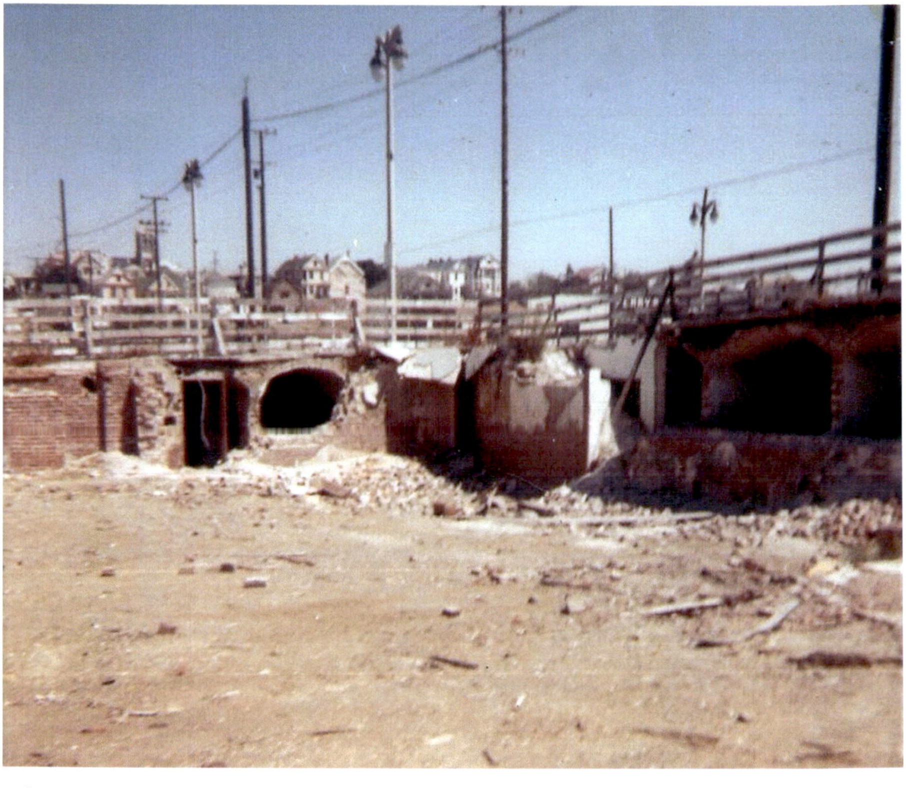

When work crews tore down the old Lynch Building on Lower Georgia Street as part of Vallejo's redevelopment project, cells were found beneath the structure. They may have been used as temporary brigs for rowdy sailors. *[Mare Island Naval Museum]*

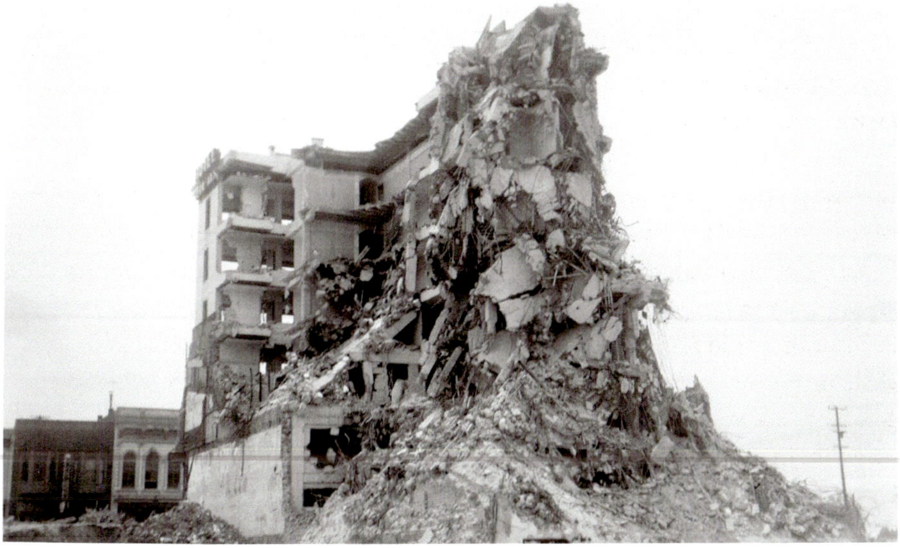

Redevelopment crews had a big job on their hands when they tore down the eight-story Hotel Georgian, at the time the tallest structure in Vallejo. *[Vallejo Naval and Historical Museum]*

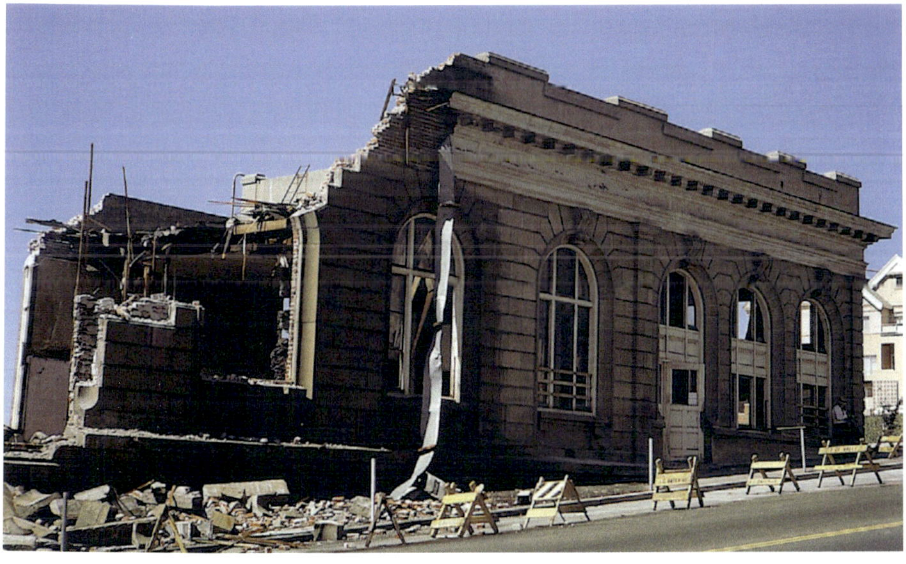

Francisco Lopez took this photograph of Vallejo's Carnegie Library while it was being demolished in 1970. It was one of the last buildings to be torn down during Vallejo's redevelopment era. *[Francisco Lopez collection]*

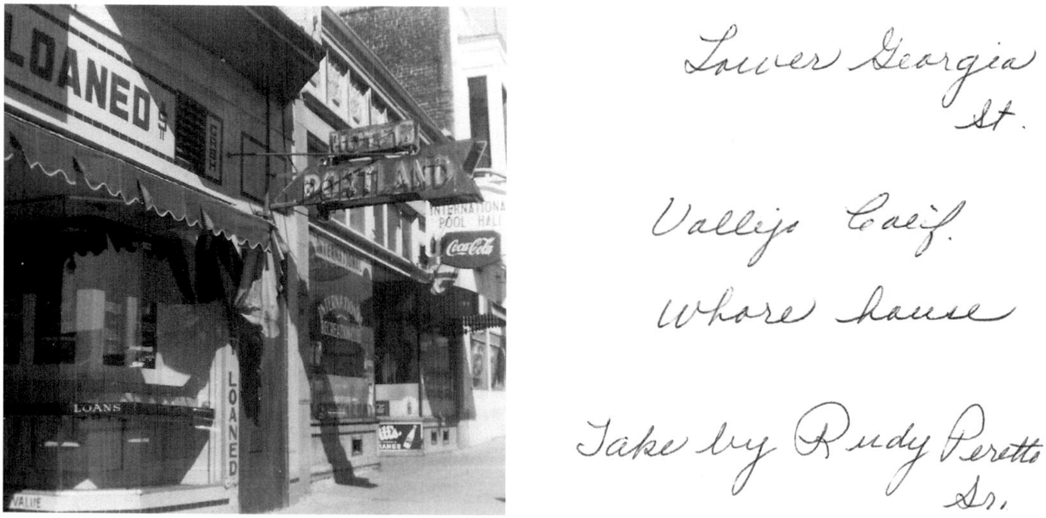

Longtime Vallejo Police Officer Rudy Peretto Jr. took this photo of the Portland Hotel on Lower Georgia Street. He labeled the hotel a whorehouse. *[Rudy Peretto Jr. collection]*

Rudy Peretto Sr., a longtime Vallejo police officer, spent many hours at various Lower Georgia demolition sites, hunting for coins, bottles and anything else that was collectible. Rudy Peretto Jr. said his father also went into some buildings in the district before they were bulldozed, salvaging pictures, signs, a chandelier and other items. In one old home, he found $20 bills taped to the bottom of several plates stacked behind a false wall. He also took photos of the buildings, including several in which brothels had been located. Peretto Sr. knew his way around the district: it was his first beat when he hired on as a policeman in the early 1950s. Peretto Jr. still has photos of the Portland, Howard, Royal and Astoria hotels, taken by his father in the early 1960s. The same words are written on the back of each hotel photo: "Lower Georgia St., Vallejo, Calif., whore house, taken by Rudy Peretto Sr." What his father saw walking the Lower Georgia beat was "unimaginable," Peretto Jr. said. "He told me there were tunnels that led from the gambling halls, so people could get out of there if the police showed up. The Georgia Street bars were open all night long, 2 a.m., 4 a.m., 6 a.m. in the morning. There were tons of sailors all the time. It was wide open."

In a June 2, 1963, column, Wyman Riley wrote again about demolition of the Lower Georgia Street district, at that point mostly complete:

> Today it is empty ground, or piles of rubble, awaiting urban renewal. As one citizen remarked, "The place looks like it was hit by The Bomb." It does, too, but what stood there is better forgotten because new and better buildings and businesses will occupy the area.

Lower Georgia street once was ablaze with neon lights (this just before and during the war years) and the street was crowded at all hours. During World War II "shills" lured customers into gambling places (45 of them in a two-block area) and bar girls competed with their professional sisters (24 establishments) for customers. It was a lively, if bawdy and illegal, stretch of the street, and a never-ending headache to military and civilian police.

Georgia Street, in the lower blocks, will never be the same. There are those who regret the fact but they are few. The majority welcome the redevelopment and look forward to the day when the entire "strip" is rejuvenated.

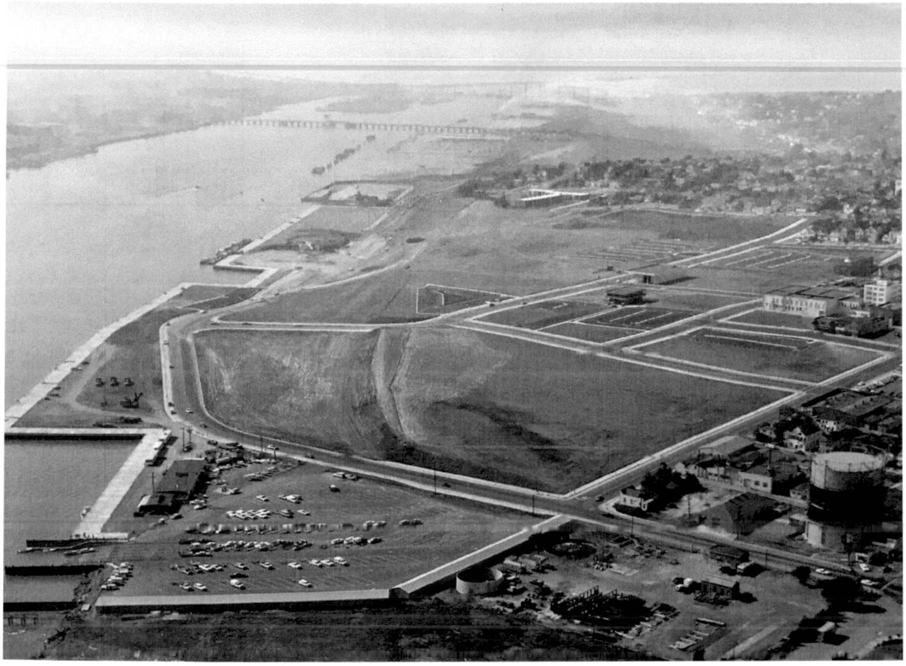

By 1970, Vallejo's massive redevelopment project had resulted in demolition of more than 500 structures in an area covering about 100 acres. Another 25 acres were added by extending the city's shoreline along Mare Island Strait. *[Vallejo Naval and Historical Museum]*

Epilogue

Vallejo's Marina Vista redevelopment project, headed by Jim Richardson, the city's redevelopment director, got off to a good start. By 1970, 533 structures had been torn down in an area covering about 100 acres. Another 25 acres were added by building a seawall in what had been a tidal zone and then backfilling earth behind the new wall. A new city hall, public library and post office was built in what had been the heart of the Lower Georgia Street district. Commercial projects and apartment construction also had started. Combined redevelopment costs at that point exceeded $20 million. But there were ominous signs, including banking as the primary commercial use and only a limited number of retail outlets to draw shoppers into the area. Of the more than 600 new apartment units constructed by 1970, nearly two-thirds were designated for low-income families. Big retailers were relocating to the new Larwin Plaza shopping center, which had been built in the early 1960s north of the old downtown. By the 1980s, major downtown businesses such as the Levees department store had closed, unable to compete against Larwin Plaza and other malls being built closer to freeways. The Mare Island Ferry Company decided in 1986 to stop running its boats that for years had hauled shipyard workers from Vallejo to Mare Island and back. It got worse in 1993 when Vallejo's true anchor, the Mare Island Naval Shipyard, was listed for closure during the federal Base Realignment and Closure process. The historic shipyard was decommissioned on April Fools' Day, 1996. That devastating blow was followed by the harsh local impact caused by the subprime mortgage crisis and collapse of the nation's housing bubble in the early 2000s. That was followed by the city's Chapter 9 bankruptcy filing in 2008, which forced a major reduction in police and other public safety workers and, not surprisingly, led to a significant increase in crime.

Despite the problems, Vallejo has persevered. Skyrocketing costs of living and doing business elsewhere in the San Francisco Bay area made the community one of the last good real estate deals in the region. New businesses opened around the city and in old Navy industrial buildings on Mare Island. A new city general plan focused on Vallejo's scenic riverfront location. Entrepreneurs sought to capitalize on the community's colorful past—and that past isn't all bad. On the positive side, Vallejo is a tough, gritty town that from its start in the early 1850s figured out how to survive and grow. There are no sure bets on Vallejo's future, but the potential is obvious. As the city moves ahead, it helps to keep in mind the slightly inexact quote attributed to Mare Island Naval Shipyard's first commandant, David Farragut, during the Civil War Battle of Mobile Bay: "Damn the torpedoes, full speed ahead."

Appendix

Below is a partial list of businesses in the Lower Georgia district from World War II to the early 1960s. Based on numerous statements and reports from government officials and agencies, there were about 100 saloons in Vallejo, mainly in the Lower Georgia district, by the early 1900s. More than 30 cardrooms and small casinos were located in basements or back rooms of the bars, and at least a couple dozen brothels were in the district, mainly in rooming houses above or near the bars. More than one name at an address indicates name changes over time, or more than one business at an address.

Georgia Street

Foot of Georgia—Mare Island Ferry Co., Skipper's Coffee Shop
36—Channel Club
47—Rafferty Cigars, Toney's Tavern
50—C. Schroeder-cigars, Jumbo Barbeque
100—C. Chantilas-restaurant, Island Club
101—D. O'Neil-liquor, Anchor Club
101A—Ritz Rooms
102—Moore Rooms
104—Navy Loan & Jewelry Co., Philippine Village
105—Navy Lunch, Focs'le
106—J. Atell Pawnbrokers, Bay Loan Office, Boston Loans
107—John Simos-restaurant, Tom Halioties-billiards
108½—Portland Hotel

110—International Recreation Club, pool hall
111—George's Grocery
112-116—Philadelphia Building
112—Fleet's Inn, J & G Café, Cora's Place
114—Franklin Hotel
115—Palm Grill
116—Forte's barber shop.
117—Jack's Place, Herman-liquor
119—Parmisano & Sons Fish Market
121—Johnny Colombo-liquor
121½—Owl Club
124—Dopey Norman's, Up 2 Date barbershop
125—Kin Fong Café
126—126 Club
126½—Brown's watch repair
128—C. Gibson Shooting Gallery
128A—Jos. Pinelli-restaurant
129—Berry May Shooting Gallery
130—Rapiman Rooms
131—R. Dunphy-liquor
131½—Coney Island Café, J. Gavecousta-restaurant
132—W. Clifford-poultry, Marvin's Place.
133—Liberty Café, W. Spatharos-liquor, record store
133B—Spot Lite Club
134—Shamrock Café, Harry Won
136—G. Cabot-restaurant, Aglipay-restaurant, Penales Café
136C—Belva Rooms, Senda Hotel
137—Naval Base Café, Palace Café, Sacramento Club, UN pool hall
138—Oriental Market
139—Glenn Rooms, Bohol Rooms
141—Three Star Café, N. Arvanitakis-liquor
142—B. Goldman pawnshop
143—Mare Island Johnny's-barber, Harbor tailors-cleaners
144 —Astor House, D. Gonas-restaurant
145—Rex Rooms, Gray Top Cab
146—North Star Cafe, A. Kypriotis-liquor
147—Naval Base Cafe
200—New York Loan, R. Davis, A. Shaffer-pawnbroker
204—Vallejo Grille, Razes-restaurant, St. Francis Rooms

205—Turf Club
206—Valmar Theater, Navy City Elks
207—Navy Café, Ben Pappas-liquor
210—C & S Sportland and Locker Club, Yvonne's lunch and pool hall
211—Brass Rail, K. Actipes-liquor, Funcade
212—R. Krueger barber
213—Grand Hotel, 4 Winds Lockers
214—Howard Loan and Jewelry, John Musso-pawnbroker
215—Rex Club
216—Sports Club, F. Buozilko-liquor, Budd's Place
216A—Howard Hotel
217—Bay City Grill, Nunn restaurant
217½ Georgia—Casino Café, J. Kallis-liquor
218—Photography, barber
218½—G. Nicholson-restaurant, Faith Rescue Mission
219—Tommy Kilbane's Porthole Cafe, A. Galley-restaurant, A. Heller-liquor
219-23—Magistrini Building
219½—Veterans Lunch, Royal Hotel
220—Shasta Rooms, J. Anthanassion-liquor
221—Al's Sport Shop
222—Shipbuilders' Café, Glaser Bros.-liquor, Lincoln Loans
222A—A. Zimos-liquor
222B—Club Tavern, Cavern
223—N. Sourbis-liquor, States Club
225—Bank Club, New Jack's, Yellow Cab
228—Georgian Hotel
229—Jack's Place, M. Thanos-liquor, Tom's Place
229½—Astoria Hotel
230—Georgian Café, Vohland-restaurant
230A—Dorshkind jeweler, Doc Webb's Trade Winds tattoos
231—Pete's Place, Puza & Gooding-liquor. Jim's Place, Turf Club
232—Farragut Club
232½—Vallejo Sports Arena
233—Solano Inn, B. Joseph-liquor
235—Lark Rooms
236—Smiling Sam's, Neal's Liquor
237—McNamee Billiards, Playland
239—Clavo Building, Crystal Hotel, Cozy Hotel, 239 Hotel
240—Brown's Stationery, Newspapers, Mann jeweler

241—D. Bithos-liquor, Golden West Café
242—Bank of America
243—Quality Café, G. Brotsis, Evans-restaurant
245—Keg Inn, Military Bottle Shop, E. Sullivan-liquor
247—Grubstick Drugs, Boll & Kilpatrick Drugs

BRANCIFORTE STREET

1—T. Brown-liquor
22—Solano Distributors-liquor
201—Service station
202—Shoe Shine
216-18—Barbers
302—Careful Cab Co.
308-10—M. Brannon-billiards, restaurant
322—D. Dearmon-restaurant
323—Knotty Pine, H. Hamilton-tavern

SANTA CLARA STREET

307—Naval YMCA
319—San Diego Café
317-21—Lee Rooms
319—J. O'Neil-liquor
323½—Rex Rooms
407—S. Geray-cigars
411—Ming's Coffee Shop
416—Lucky Sun Market
417—Eagle Café
427—Manx Grill
426—Empress Hotel
427—G. Potter-liquor
428—Original Barrel House
508—Bon Ton Apts.
515—Astor Café
518—John's Place, Bob's Place
519—Lucky's Place

SACRAMENTO STREET

319—Nordstrom Hotel
323½—Rex Rooms
427—Seevel Apartments
509½—Commercial Hotel
518—Salvation Army, hotel, store
524—Spanish-American deli
525—Dutch's Club
527—Stephens Rooms

VIRGINIA STREET

100—Traveler's Café, Cotton Club
101—Victory Corner
104—Capitol Hotel
106—Swede's Hut
111—Nick's Place, Nell's Place
120—Virginia Court Apts.
121—Porru's Place, Bon Gusto Cafe
141—J. Lukes-beer distributor
144—Astor House-hotel, restaurant
200—Vallejo Distributors-liquor
203—Tintorri grocery
239—Lido Café
241—Union hall, rooming house
244—Carnegie Library
324—Three-Two-Four Club
326—Jay Bozeman-billiards
328—Vallejo Hotel
329—Marval Theater
331—Rio Theater
339—Relay-liquor

Bibliography

Allen, Robert L., *The Port Chicago Mutiny* (New York, Amistad Press, 1993)

Burrough, Bryan, *Public Enemies* (New York, Penguin Books, 2004)

Conforte, Joe, and Toll, David, *Breaks, Brains & Balls* (Gold Hill, Gold Hill Publishing, 2011)

Cullen, Gary, *The Boys From Boston* (Vallejo, Gary Cullen, 2015)

Eldredge, Zoeth Skinner, *The Beginnings of San Francisco* (San Francisco, Zoeth S. Eldredge, 1912)

Grant, Edwin, "Report of Vice Investigation at Vallejo and Benicia and Vicinity in Solano County, California" (College Park, National Archives, 1917)

Guttridge, Leonard F., *Mutiny: A History of Naval Insurrection* (Annapolis, Naval Institute Press, 2006)

Hubbard, Harry D., *Vallejo* (Boston, Meador Publishing, 1941)

Johnson, Bascom, "Report on Conditions Surrounding the Naval station at Mare Island, California" (College Park, National Archives, 1917)

Kern, James E., *Images of America: Vallejo* (Charleston, Arcadia Publishing, 2004)

Leach, Frank A., *Recollections of a Newspaperman: A Record of Life and Events in California* (San Francisco, Samuel Levinson, 1917)

Lemmon, Sue, and Wichels, E. D., *Sidewheelers to Nuclear Power* (Annapolis, Leeward Publications, 1977)

Lott, Arnold S., *A Long Line of Ships* (Annapolis, United States Naval Institute, 1954)

MacGregor, Morris J., *Integration of the Armed Forces, 1940-1965* (Washington, D. C., Center of Military History, 1981)

McGriff-Payne, Sharon, *Images of America: African Americans in Vallejo* (Charleston, Arcadia Publishing, 2012)

Moore, William Howard, *The Kefauver Committee and the Politics of Crime* (Columbia, University of Missouri Press, 1974)

Nagle, Jimmy Albert, *The Unholy Three* (New York, Vantage Press, 1975)

Nickel, Steven and Helmer, William J., *Baby Face Nelson: Portrait of a Public Enemy* (Nashville, Cumberland House Publishing, 2002)

Okrent, Daniel, *Last Call: The Rise and Fall of Prohibition* (New York, Scribner, 2010)

Oxford, June, *The Capital That Couldn't Stay Put* (San Diego, June Oxford, 1983)

Ramsey Jr., William R., "Reports of Special Agent W.R. Ramsey Jr., Jan. 22, 1935 and May 10, 1934" (San Francisco, FBI reports produced in the trial of individuals charged with harboring Baby Face Nelson.)

Rosenus, Alan, *General Vallejo and the Advent of the Americans* (Berkeley, Heyday Books, 1995)

Sheinkin, Steve, *The Port Chicago 50: Disaster, Mutiny, and the Fight for Civil Rights* (New York, Roaring Brook Press, 2014)

Smith, Alice; Anderson, Ivy; Angus, Devon, Alice, *Memoirs of a Barbary Coast Prostitute* (Berkeley, Heyday Books, 2016)

Solano Historian, various issues (Vallejo, Solano County Historical Society)

Spooner, C. W., *Yeah, What Else? Essays, Memoirs, Poems, and Reviews* (Bloomington, iUniverse, 2016)

Truman, Harry S, Executive Order 9981 and related documents (Independence, Harry S. Truman Library & Museum)

U.S. Senate Special Committee to Investigate Organized Crime in Interstate Commerce, Hearing Reports, Part 2, June 22-23, June 28, July 6-7, Aug. 16, 1950 (Washington, D.C., U.S. Government Printing Office)

Vallejo newspaper articles and columns and related materials on Vallejo from other U.S. newspapers, the *Associated Press* and *United Press International.*

Vallejo Naval and Historical Museum files and Mare Island Museum files relating to Lower Georgia district.

Watterson, Rodney K., *Whips to Walls: Naval Discipline from Flogging to Progressive Era Reform at Portsmouth Prison* (Annapolis, Naval Institute Press, 2014)

Widenmann family records (Green Valley, Dr. Charles Widenmann)

Acknowledgments

This book may not have been written had it not been for the drawings and paintings of longtime Vallejo artist Dorothy Herger that represent the only full record of the Lower Georgia Street district. Her art kept alive the colorful history of the district long after every building there had been bulldozed. I asked Dorothy why she made this effort and she replied: "In the 1960s, the destruction of Lower Georgia Street began. I was intrigued by the history of my home town and the contrasting visual richness of the Barbary Coast. Brendan, how could I not record a history of Vallejo that was about to disappear?" Thanks to Dorothy, this book is enlivened by many of those images.

As mentioned in the introduction, I relied on stories that ran in newspapers in Vallejo, other San Francisco Bay area cities and elsewhere around the country. Much of the information for the book wasn't to be found elsewhere in printed form, and the people with first-hand knowledge of some of the events were long gone.

My parents, Wyman and Marjorie Riley, both journalists and writers, years ago sparked my interest in the Lower Georgia Street district, by columns and articles they wrote and by stories they would tell at home. Their columns that dealt with the Lower Georgia Street district provided me with valuable material.

Historian Jim Kern, executive director of the Vallejo Naval and Historical Museum, provided me with full access to the museum's research library, archives and photo collections and, most importantly, brought his extensive knowledge of Vallejo history to bear in reading and editing my draft copy.

Photographer Rick Mariani, who has done extensive photographic work for the museum, made high-quality reproductions of Dorothy Herger's art and of numerous historic images that illustrate the book.

Many other current and former Vallejoans contributed to the book, some with their own memories dating to World War II and even earlier. Others, whose families have been in Vallejo for generations, shared stories that had been told to them by their parents and grandparents.

Serving on a Navy ship from 1968 to 1970, I heard more stories about Lower Georgia Street from older crewmembers, "lifers" who had been in the Navy and on liberty in Vallejo when the city's "Barbary Coast" was going strong. Other World War II Navy vets who met from time to time at the Vallejo Naval and Historical Museum also told me their stories.

My Never Sweats writing group friends, especially Carol Jensen, Michael Fischer and David Toll, encouraged me with their love of history and by sharing information developed in their own research.

Maggie Tracey, my spouse, was my main source of encouragement. She read every word I wrote, with a good editor's eye and with high interest. I couldn't have completed this without her.